THE
SPY
TEST

JOEL JESSUP

THE SPY TEST

USE YOUR WITS
AND TRADECRAFT TO
SOLVE THE PUZZLES

IVY PRESS

Quarto

First published in 2024 by Ivy Press
an imprint of The Quarto Group.
One Triptych Place, London, SE1 9SH
United Kingdom
T (0)20 7700 6700
www.Quarto.com

A catalogue record for this book is available from
the British Library.

ISBN 978-0-71129-820-0
Ebook ISBN 978-0-71129-821-7

Design by Dave Jones
Senior Art Editor Renata Latipova
Publisher Richard Green
Editor Jennifer Barr
Puzzle Consultant John Jessup
Illustrations by Emma Fraser Reid
Production Manager Rohana Yusof

Printed in the UK
10 9 8 7 6 5 4 3 2 1

Contents

Introduction

Welcome to *The Spy Test*, a puzzle book that takes you on an immersive journey through the intriguing world of espionage. Divided into three sections – Recruitment, Training and In the Field – each segment simulates a critical phase of a spy's career through a series of puzzles that will challenge your intellect, sharpen your instincts and ignite your imagination.

Recruitment

Here, you will encounter puzzles designed to test your logical reasoning, observational skills and problem-solving abilities. These challenges include deciphering coded messages, identifying patterns and mastering the art of deduction.

Training

Once recruited, the next phase is Training. In this section, you'll delve deeper into the craft of espionage, honing the skills necessary to operate effectively in the field. Training is where theory meets practice, and you will encounter a variety of challenges designed to build your competence and confidence.

The puzzles in this section focus on developing key spy skills, such as cryptography, stealth and surveillance. You'll tackle complex ciphers, practice your ability to blend into different environments and refine your capacity for gathering intelligence discreetly. Additionally, this section

----

explores the psychological aspects of espionage, including the importance of maintaining a cover identity and managing stress under pressure.

In the Field

By the time you complete the Training section, you will have a well-rounded skill set, equipped to handle the dynamic and unpredictable nature of espionage work. The puzzles will have tested your patience, precision, and perseverance, essential traits for any successful spy.

The final section, In the Field, simulates the high-stakes reality of a spy's life, where every decision can have significant consequences. Here, you will apply all the skills you have acquired in scenarios that challenge your ability to think on your feet and adapt to rapidly changing situations. Puzzles in this section involve real-world spy operations, requiring you to infiltrate secure locations, communicate with other agents using clandestine methods and gather critical intelligence. These tasks are designed to test your strategic thinking and decision-making under pressure, reflecting the complexities and dangers faced by spies in the field.

Prepare to embark on a journey that will challenge your mind, thrill your senses, and perhaps even reveal your inner spy.

PART ONE

Recruitment

Recruitment

This section demonstrates recruitment techniques used by espionage agencies, concentrating on the methods designed to find people to work in a professional capacity as a field agent, information officer or some other official role.

Over the centuries the type of person or set of skills needed for espionage work has shifted based on social, geopolitical and even scientific developments. Early agents were often merchants, diplomats, or sometimes sailors, as they had the means and reason to travel at a time when travel was expensive and unusual. This technique was used by Queen Elizabeth I who had an extensive spy network used to track and manipulate various plots and intrigues.

As travel technology advanced, it became more possible for everyone to traverse countries and oceans more easily, which meant that agents could be recruited from a wider range of backgrounds. They could be political insiders with useful connections or even criminals with experience in deception and larceny, motivated by political ideology, or

---

morally flexible. In the early twentieth century many agents were approached at university because of their social connections.

During the Second World War, the increasing importance of codebreaking led to some more innovative attempts at recruitment. On 13 January 1942 the *Daily Telegraph* ran a particularly challenging crossword developed by the finest minds at Bletchley Park. Anyone who could solve it in less than 12 minutes was encouraged to get in contact as prospective codebreakers for Bletchley Park. Later in the twentieth century agencies sought to try and bring in people from more diverse backgrounds and it was often suspected that mysterious advertisements which appeared in innocuous publications were in fact breadcrumbs to lead insightful individuals into the clandestine services.

The ever-shifting political and technological landscape requires an ever-wider net to be cast, and this chapter gives an idea of the different ways agents might have been recruited.

1: The empty chairs

The numbers along the top and side indicate how many cells in each row or column must be filled in or left blank. By cross referencing horizontal and the vertical, you will be able to work out which boxes should be coloured in. This will then leave a route towards one of the chairs.

Which chair can you reach?

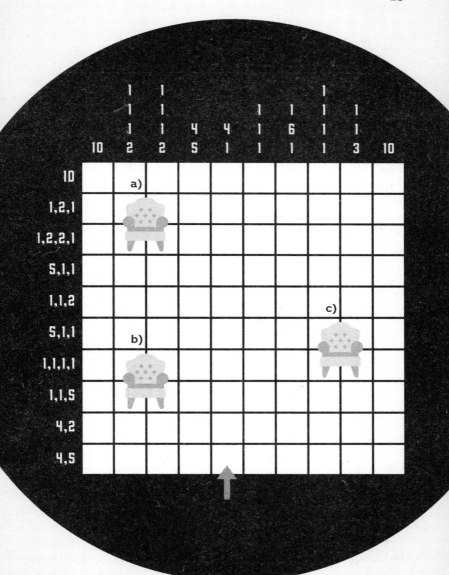

2: Advice column

Ask the psychic

Dear Psychic,
I've been seeing a young lady for three months, but two weeks ago I learned I have a love rival… one who claims he can predict the future!

I went to confront him at his antiques stall and found him smiling smugly surrounded by dozens of knick-knacks. I cast doubt on his supposed abilities, so he asked me to pick a number between one and twenty.

"Tell me the number," he said.

"It's fourteen!" I replied, "I thought you were psychic."

"I can't read minds, only the future. I knew you'd pick that number. Look in this magic box," he said, pointing at one on the shelf behind him. I looked inside and found a piece of paper on which he had written "I knew you'd pick fourteen!"

I was chilled to the bone. How did he know?

Yours, KP in Chiswick

The psychic says

Dear KP, this man is clearly blessed with the gift of foresight. But that does not make him better than you. Buy your young lady a gift, to give her the foresight to know her future is with you!

From information revealed in the letter, how did the love rival predict the number?

3: Pop-up

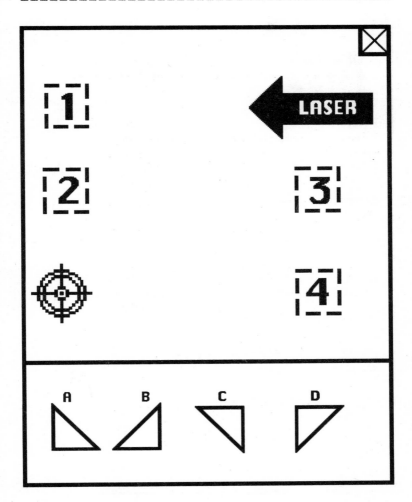

If the laser travels in a straight line, where can you put the four mirrors labelled A, B, C and D to make five?

4: Job advertisment

INTELLIGENT OUTDOOR WORKERS WITH OVER 15 YEARS' EXPERIENCE

Wanted for temporary position as clerical assistant in sales department of successful paper company in Scotland.

Position is permanent, hours 9pm–5:30am, would suit young people looking for the experience.

Excellent working facilities, pay begins at $3,000 a day. Mongeese welcome.

Applications should be made to:
MIJS Pharmaceuticals Ltd,
14 Belchester Close,
Swansea,
Wales

Identify the ten incosistencies or errors in this advert.

5: The hourglass riddle

A GLASSMAKER CAME to a kingdom where every citizen had an hourglass they used to measure the time of every activity. He went to the king and declared:

"Your hourglasses are flawed. They cannot measure time accurately. When you turn them over, it is inevitable that some grains of sand will remain in the upper bulb."

The man offered to teach the king's glassmakers how to make glass so perfectly smooth that not a single grain would remain in the upper bulb, and the king readily agreed.

Soon it was done and all of the hourglasses in the kingdom kept perfect time. But when the glassmaker asked the king for his payment, the king instead led him to an underground chamber where there was a huge glass silo filled with sand.

"You think you are cleverer than I," said the king. "Well, this is where we are keeping all the sand for the hourglasses. It is built from the same glass you have taught us to make."

The king demonstrated, removing the stopper at the base of the silo and filling an hourglass with sand, before closing it up.

"Now, wise man, tell me how many grains of sand there are in this silo. If you are correct, I will give you all the gold in my treasury. But if you are wrong, I will have you sealed up inside the silo forever."

The glassmaker turned pale.

"How long do I have?" he asked.

"Take as long as you like." said the King. "But the answer cannot be 'some' or 'many'. It must be definitive."

The glassmaker thought carefully. And then, after a while, he was able to give the King a correct answer, and walked away with all the kingdom's gold.

How did the glassmaker give the King the correct answer?

6: Join the dots

Even the least experienced puzzler can solve this odd little conundrum!

How can you join the dots to create two images? Once the shapes have been found, work out how they can fit together to form one of the images on the following page.

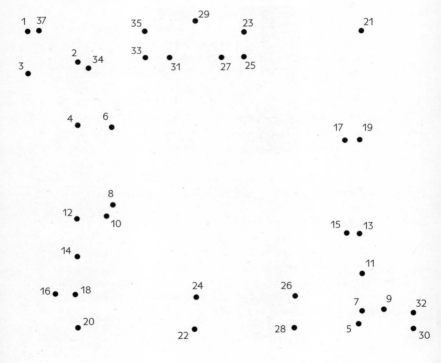

a)

b)

c)

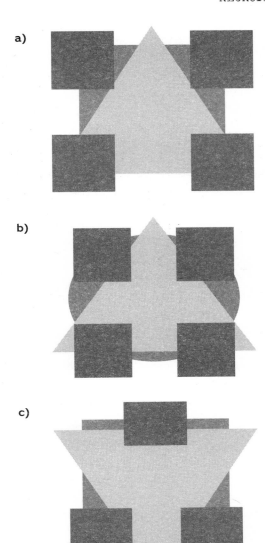

7: Magazine advertisement

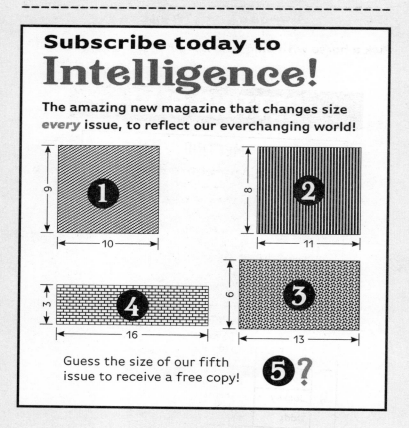

Using logic and maths, work out what the size of the fifth issue should be.

8: Betting odds

Pick a horse with unique odds and a unique name.

BETTING SLIP

MEETING
Chesterton Apprentice Plate 1996

1	Horse	**MARIGOLD DREAMER**
	Jockey	*G Hancock*
	Odds	**20/4 fav**
2	Horse	**AMBER DRAGON**
	Jockey	*R Keddridge*
	Odds	**5/1**
3	Horse	**SAPPHIRE LIGHT**
	Jockey	*L McKeen*
	Odds	**10/2**
4	Horse	**MAJOR MUSTARD**
	Jockey	*H Frost*
	Odds	**6/2**
5	Horse	**EMERALD ISLE**
	Jockey	*D O'Malley*
	Odds	**15/3**
6	Horse	**SCARLET ROSE**
	Jockey	*M Neeson*
	Odds	**20/5**

Cyphers and Cryptography

Information is the currency that intelligence agencies deal in, so being able to keep these pieces of lucrative material secret is the priority. The codes and cryptology used by today's intelligence services have been centuries in the making.

In a Caesar cypher, a single letter is the key, assigned to A. For example, something encoded with F as the key would have A=F, B=G, C=H etc. If the codebreaker hasn't been given the key, they can instead look for a phrase they would expect to find in the message and work out how many places the letters shift on based on that.

An extension of this is the Vigenère cypher in which each letter of your plain text is encoded differently based on a different letter key which is usually part of a phrase. For example, if your message was THANK YOU and the key phrase is COVER, the first letter T would be encoded using a cypher where A=C,

Caesar cypher

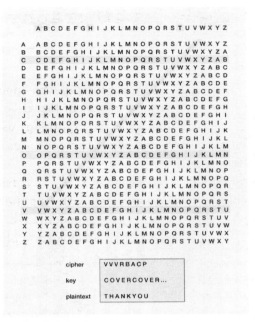

Vigenère cipher

the first letter of COVER. This would make B=D, C=E, D=F, so T would equal V as everything is shifted on by two spaces. The H, the second letter of THANKYOU would be encoded using the cypher A=O as the is the second letter of COVER and so on. To decode, you would be given the code phrase/word (in this case COVER) and would simply reverse the process. The first letter of the message V would move back two spaces to give you T, and so on. If the message you want to encrypt is longer than the code key/phrase, then you would simply keep repeating the key (eg COVERCOVER).

9: Spy movie poster

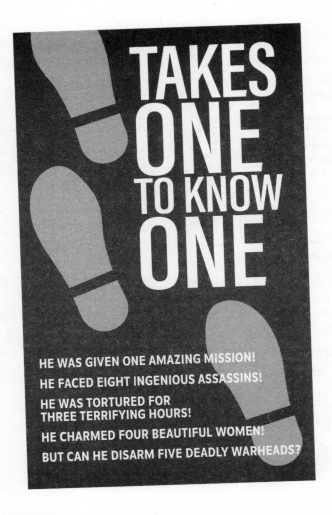

TAKES ONE TO KNOW ONE

HE WAS GIVEN ONE AMAZING MISSION!
HE FACED EIGHT INGENIOUS ASSASSINS!
HE WAS TORTURED FOR THREE TERRIFYING HOURS!
HE CHARMED FOUR BEAUTIFUL WOMEN!
BUT CAN HE DISARM FIVE DEADLY WARHEADS?

What is the secret three digit number hidden within this poster? Remember – to find the right answer, you need positive attitude!

10: Doorbells

LOCAL IMPORTS *If no answer, ring bell for JB* ○	**VACANT** ○
Jean Bertrand **Night watchman,** DO NOT RING BEFORE 7PM! ○	**Jane Burlington** (BELL BROKEN, RING DENTIST'S BELL) ○
Gloria I **Reynolds-** **Caretaker** ○	GARETH INSKIP, **Podiatrist** NO LONGER AT THIS ADDRESS ○
Dr Arthur Heritage DDS *(IF AFTER 6,* *PLEASE RING GI)* ○	**JAMES BENTON** **INSURANCE** (Unavailable after 5pm) ○
DR AYDEN WILTON ○	**LO-CAL** **IMPORTERS** Artificial sweeteners and diet food. ○

**If you are told to arrive at 6:30pm and make contact
with Local Imports but find that pressing their buzzer
receives no answer, which buzzer should you press?**

11: The Koan Card

There were **12** groups.

They were all animals of
different species and manner.

13 Cats,   **35** pigs,   **64** dogs,   **42** birds.

All equal in stature. If a man were to tell

57 lies and   **76** truths

Who should lead?

Find the links between the numbers on the Koan cards, connecting like to like, to decide whether you should go through the door on the left, right or straight on. Which one is the correct one?

12: Crime prevention leaflet

Can you spot the six secret observers hidden in this leaflet?

Morse Code

In the early nineteenth century the development of
electronic communications saw the need for a simple,
non-secret code, transmittable and easily deciphered by
the recipient. In 1837 Samuel Morse invented what we
know now as International Morse Code, using the electrical
pulses in a series of dots and dashes to represent the
Latin alphabet. It was often used by the military to
communicate, and proved vital during the Second World
War as radiotelegraphy using Morse Code was used to send
messages between warships and patrol planes and
their bases.

While this code was well known, it gave spies behind
enemy line the opportunity to quickly communicate
their messages using a combination of Morse Code and
an encryption on easily concealed telecommunication
devices. Suddenly secret communication could be
very quick.

Foolproof encryption devices were the aim of both sides
in the Second World War, and the most famous of these,
the Germans Enigma machine (see page xx), was broken
by cryptologists at Bletchley Park. But in more recent
times advances in computer science have taken cyphers
and cryptology beyond the understanding of most
humans, with end-to-end encryption vital for almost all
businesses and nations. But electronic surveillance and
code-cracking has also made sending secret messages
ever more difficult...

Morse Code letters

A	• —	J	• — — —	S	• • •	
B	— • • •	K	— • —	T	—	
C	— • — •	L	• — • •	U	• • —	
D	— • •	M	— —	V	• • • —	
E	•	N	— •	W	• — —	
F	• • — •	O	— — —	X	— • • —	
G	— — •	P	• — — •	Y	— • — —	
H	• • • •	Q	— — • —	Z	— — • •	
I	• •	R	• — •			

Morse Code numbers

1	• — — — —	6	— • • • •
2	• • — — —	7	— — • • •
3	• • • — —	8	— — — • •
4	• • • • —	9	— — — — •
5	• • • • •	0	— — — — —

13: Want to be a spy?

What is the hidden code?

.. ..-. -.-- --- ..- .- .-. . -. --

WANT TO BE A SPY?

We're looking for ambitious people who enjoy challenges and international travel to join our growing team of undercover agents.

Tuxedo and gun provided, cocktails and casino chips standard issue.

Do you enjoy underwater combat and rappelling into volcanoes? Can you drive cars quickly while dodging gunfire?

If you can find out how to contact us, this is the job for you!

-..- --- ..--. --- .-. - -.- . -. - -.-

14: Letter to the editor

SIR,

I noticed several obvious errors in your article dated the 10th of June, regarding the recent archaeological excavations in Arizona, USA.

1. It claimed the capital city of Arizona is Tucson, when it is in fact Phoenix.

2. It said Dr Hanley's "copper digging tools" were kept dry to prevent rust. Copper does not rust.

3. Dr Hanley is quoted to say "It can be uncomfortable working in 85 degree weather." At 85 degrees Celsius human beings would quickly expire, not be merely "uncomfortable"!

4. The article claims there are no lakes in Arizona. There are at least 128 lakes in Arizona.

5. The article asserts that the dig will have to close on the 30th of February next year, but there is no such date.

Which of these errors is actually not an error?

15: Shop window cards

As long as you follow the clues (and know where to start!) these cards in a shop window can lead you to the place you need to go and you will ultimately find a new contact.

Which of these cards will lead you to a new contact?

Looking for a fresh start?

SANDERSON'S GROCERS need weekend workers. Located to the right of this newsagents.

FOR SALE

Vauxhall Cavalier. Good condition, one careful owner, all papers. Straight cash only.

FRANK REDDINGTON: FISHMONGER.
HERRING, COD AND TROUT
FRESH EVERYDAY

CORNWELL ANTIQUES

Curios and artefacts of a bygone age, quality porcelain and high grade silver. Fair offers made for authentic items

ROOF RESCUE
PROBLEMS WITH A LEAKY OR OLD ROOF?
We'll be glad to get up there and solve your problems!

RON'S ROOFING

- Tiles
- Insulation
- Brickwork
- Repointing.

TO LET
DOWNSTAIRS FLAT

En suite bathroom,
bedroom, kitchen,
close to Tube.

MISSING
GREEN PATTERNED UMBRELLA

with carved wooden handle
resembling duck's head.

OLD VINYL?
CASSETTE TAPES?

Take them down to
Bob's Basement Records
to exchange them!

STAFF NEEDED

Southdown Café needs
Waiters and Waitresses.
Flexible hours.
Experience not required.

*You too
could
advertise
here!*

EXPERIENCED DRIVING INSTRUCTOR
SEEKS NEW STUDENTS.

FOR SALE

STAIRLIFT. In good
condition, but only goes
down, not up. Otherwise
perfect for use.

LOOKING FOR SOMETHING TO DO?

Why not visit
Port Street
Optics Museum?

LEFT HANDED?

We can provide
scissors, tools,
anything you need.
Contact us for a catalogue.
DEFT LEFTIES

PART TWO

Training

Training

Once accepted into the role of an agent, individuals underwent extensive training to hone their skills. Before the twentieth century much training would be on the job but the First and Second World Wars underlined the necessity for an active, professionally qualified intelligence agency and many training schools were established to this end. The location of many of these places remains secret but some are known, for example the CIA's Camp Peary, colloquially known as The Farm. Often, they are held in de facto locations and moved frequently.

The training given to new agents is extensive and broad. Discipline, an understanding of their role and preparedness for a variety of different scenarios are a priority. New recruits also need a good grounding in the area of their prospective operations and its geo-political and sociological significance. While some field agents need to be active and physically fit, this isn't the case for

----

everyone, as some agents are more effective if they are
believed to be less capable in this area. Being able to
observe and analyze accurately and with insight is more
important.

As modern espionage has advanced, knowledge of
cryptology techniques, such as codebreaking, has grown in
importance. More practical skills, like the ability to break
into houses or crack safes, still have relevance but in a
digital age sometimes more damage can be done with the
press of a button than with a secret midnight raid.

Training will also be given in the use of specialist
equipment, such as listening devices, as well as possibly
some information on weapons and hand-to-hand combat.
But the key lesson at the heart of all of these skills is
learning not to make assumptions and develop the
lateral thinking abilities that enable you to anticipate
the unexpected.

16: Number response

An enemy agent has been captured. You have found records of their two previous communications with their handler:

Handler:
Three Four Four One Eight.
Seagulls have been seen on the beach.
Have you packed up your picnic?

Enemy agent:
5 4 4 3 5.
The seagulls are distracted by a dead seal.
Picnic can continue for a while.

Handler:
Five Nine Two Four One.
Pack up the picnic now, the dead seal is still alive.

Enemy agent:
4 4 3 4 3.
Packing up picnic, see you back at the beach-house.

Their handler has now sent the following message:

Handler:
Six Five Eight Three Two.
Did not find you at beach-house. Have the seagulls eaten everything?

You want to respond:

'Seagulls have left area to find different beach, will unpack picnic again soon.'

Which numbers should you write before the message?

a) 2 3 8 5 6.
b) 5 4 4 3 5.
c) 3 4 3 4 4.
d) 3 4 5 5 3.
e) 2 4 3 4 2.

17: Safe word

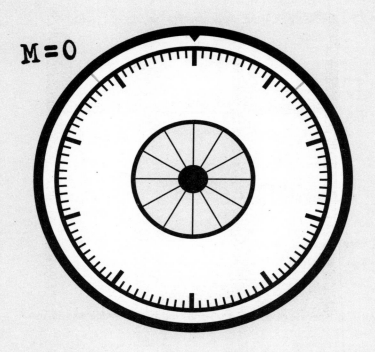

M=0

Using the knowledge that the combination to the safe is **NEVER** and the fact that the dial seems to have a scratch 12 notches along on the left side, and 13 notches along on the right as you face the dial, and you can see, "M=0" written just above the dial, **how do you turn the dial in order to unlock the safe?**

18: Keypad

Using the following information work out what the numbers on the keypad should be:

- No number is in the position it would normally occupy
- 8 is to the left of its usual position
- 4 is above 8
- 7 is not next to 8
- Working diagonally, the top corner number minus the number at the centre equals the bottom corner number.
- No line has only odd or even numbers.

19: Defuse the bomb

As part of a training exercise you need to learn how to disarm a fake bomb by cutting the correct wire, which is the one that is attached to the detonator sticking out of the right hand side.

There are several small junction boxes where two wires enter and leave, marked with either a CIRCLE or a TRIANGLE.

One symbol indicates the wires pass straight through.

The other symbol indicates that lines cross over inside the box.

You don't know which symbol indicates which outcome. But you do know that wires cannot cross in the same box twice.

Which wire must you cut?

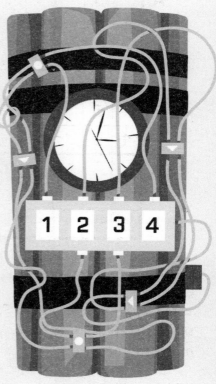

20: Connected nodes

----

1 2 3 4 5

6 7 8 9

A		3			1			5		**A**
B	4			5		7	2		3	**B**
C	2			3		4	7	6		**C**
D	8	7		9	6	1	4	3	5	**D**
E		6			5					**E**
F	1	9		4					7	**F**
G				1		9	5			**G**
H	7		1	8	3	5	9			**H**
I	5			6	7	2	3		8	**I**

You need to connect two different circuits to bypass a security system.

The only guide you have been given is this sudoku, and the image aboove it of the type of wire connection each number forms.

Which two letters can form the unbroken connection?

21: The hidden signal

You are trapped in enemy territory and waiting for
notification from HQ about when to launch a vital
operation. But your usual lines of communication have
been compromised so you fall back on emergency
measures. Every day, at 2:05 pm, a radio announcer will
say a particular sentence and this will be the cue to
launch the operation.

Day 1 - Mr. Arnold Fenchurch
"Don't forget to feed the cat!"

Day 2 - Mrs. Emily Sitwell
"Don't forget to feed the cat!"

Day 3 - Mr. Roger Hargraves
"Don't forget to feed the cat!"

Day 4 - Mrs. Rebecca Smith
"Don't forget to feed the cat!"

Day 5 - Mr. Peter Ford
"Don't forget to feed the cat!"

- -

Day 6 - Mr. Clive Dickinson
"Don't forget to feed the cat!"

- -

Day 7 - Mrs. Enid Brown
"Don't forget to feed the cat!"

- -

Day 8 - Mr. Keith Jones
"Don't forget to feed the cat!"

- -

Day 9 - Mrs. Kate Johnson
"Don't forget to feed the cat!"

- -

Day 10 - Mr. Oliver Remington
"Don't forget to feed the cat!"

- -

Keeping in mind that it could not happen on the first day, and that the name of the announcer was not said, when did you launch the operation?

22: Minefield

You are given a ten by nine of numbers which you are told
represents a minefield that blocks the escape route of some
dissidents you have to help escape from a oppressive regime.

The only clues are the entry point and three other squares,
one is a mine and the others represents a **prime** spot to
place a foot and not get blown up.

= Mine   = Safe

99	11	28	42	1	66	15	50	36	25
27	49	3	26	45	6	62	14	58	34
74	73	8	46	18	68	12	56	75	22
10	40	47	19	21	48	9	63	16	15
100	64	30	7	82	23	71	20	44	77
76	39	52	98	89	60	91	13	84	38
25	90	57	4	32	65	51	33	79	93
94	35	85	54	80	78	17	5	81	72
70	88	24	92	96	61	86	95	69	87

Which 13 squares are safe to step on?

23: Find the file

U
Y

You must break the following code to find out which file you must steal from the archives of the government office that you have infiltrated.

Any information you need to crack the cypher are available to you on this page.

N
I

F
O

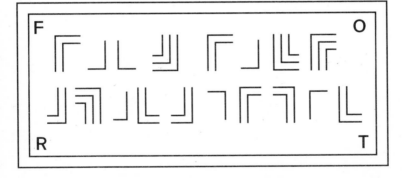

R
T

E
H

Which file must you steal from the archives?

L
D

Bletchley Park

In 1938 Admiral Sir Hugh Sinclair, then head of the Secret Intelligence Service (SIS or MI6), realized that breaking the enemy's communication systems would be key to turning the likely upcoming war to the Allies' favour. He used his own money to purchase Bletchley Park, a Victorian country estate nestled in the Buckinghamshire countryside. It became the base for the Government Code and Cypher School (GC&CS). The moment war was declared the recruitment process began, firstly by personal recommendation, then by scouring the universities of Oxford and Cambridge. They also ran a crossword competition through the *Daily Telegraph* where the best entrants were approached about making a "contribution to the war effort". Commander Alastair Denniston, operational head of the SIS, assembled a team

of code-breakers including Joan Clarke, Hugh Alexander, Bill Tutte, Stuart Milner-Barry and Alan Turing. Women made up seventy-five percent of Bletchley's workforce.

Bletchley was also home to Colossus, regarded as the world's first programmable, electronic digital computer. But it was the Bombe, Alan Turing's electromechanical device, that made the most telling contribution to deciphering the German encrypted signals by cracking the German Enigma code, a breakthrough widely believed to have shortened the war by two to three years.

Code-breaking operations came to an end at Bletchley Park in 1946 but the activities there were shrouded in secrecy and its role in winning the Second World War for the Allies was only truly revealed in the 1970s.

Bletchley Park's appearance was suitably unremarkable and its location in Buckinghamshire was conveniently central for staff and operations.

24: Frequency analysis

When signals are combined, any waves in phase with each other increase their amplitude (height), and any waves out of phase decrease it.

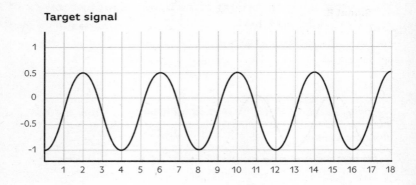

Target signal

Based on this information, which two signals need to be combined to make the target signal?

Signal A

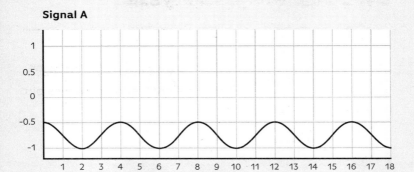

Signal B

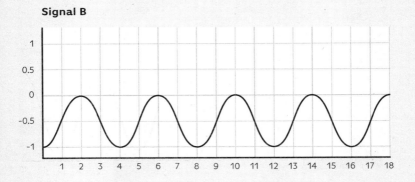

Signal C

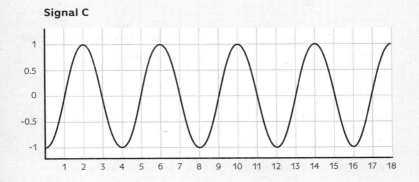

25: Find the micro cameras

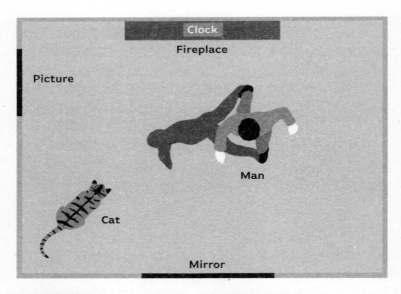

Four micro cameras are placed in a room. They may be microscopic in size and therefore very hard to find with the naked eye, but they are incredibly powerful and capable of taking incredibly detailed pictures.

From the pictures taken by the cameras, work out where the cameras are hidden.

26: A suitable code

You have to pass the access code to a secret
communication channel to one of your assets quickly
in a busy street.

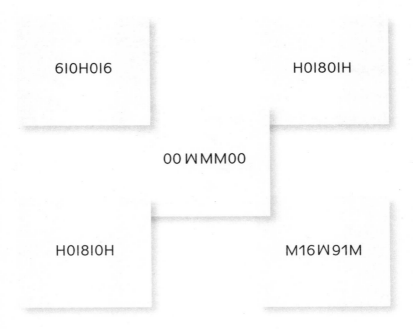

6I0H0I6

H0I80IH

00 WMM00

H0I8I0H

M16W91M

**Which of the numbers above should you choose as the
code number?**

27: Destination codewheel

Q-Z-L-S-X
Z-S-S-X-Q
Q-Q-L-S-L
S-L-L-Z-L
L-X-X-L-S
Q-X-X-X-S
Z-Z-L-S-X
L-L-Q-Q-S
X-S-L-X-L
Z-Z-S-Z-L
X-X-L

You are given a coded message and a code wheel and told it will reveal the name of a city. If you use the codewheel in the usual way, the message doesn't make sense. Would counting the letters help?

How can you use the code wheel to decode the message on the left to reveal the name of the city?

28: Anonymity

The head of your section gives you a mission that requires stealth and cunning.

You are to observe an enemy agent by waiting in the lobby of the hotel where he is staying. You are unknown to him, and have a number of possible disguise elements:

- Sunglasses
- Large hat
- Smaller beanie hat
- False bushy beard
- Large false moustache
- Blonde wig
- Or something else?

You must make a considered decision about how best to preserve your anonymity and remain undetected.

What do you choose to wear?

29: Take a shot

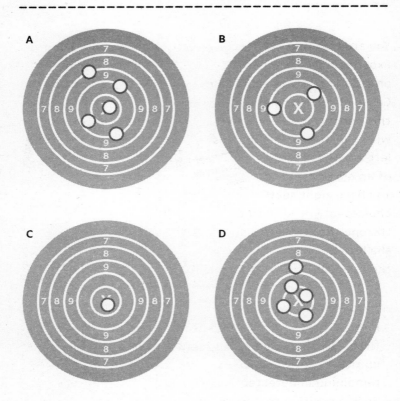

Four agents have been told to hone their skills at the shooting range and use five shots to hit their target. This is the result of the agents' shots and there were no misses.

Based on the images above who is the best shot?

30: Seat plan

You are told there is an
experienced counter agent
on a flight from Istanbul to
Cairo. All you know about
this enemy is that he walks
with a distinctive limp in his
left leg, the result
of an old war wound.
You have eight seat
choices and need to find
the one that will give you
the best chance to do
the following:

- See and identify your
  rival as he leaves the
  flight in Cairo to walk
  up the gangway whilst
  remaining undetected
- Be in a position to
  follow him.

Key: Counter agent ◯
     Occupied seats **X**

Which seat do you choose?

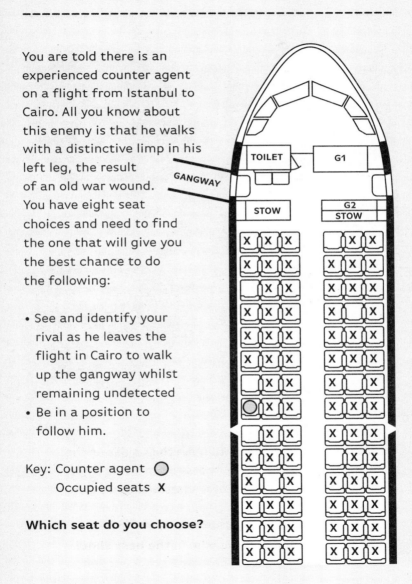

31: Sector assignment

This is an image of an enemy sector taken during an aerial reconnaissance mission. For it to be safely transmitted to you, the image had to be cut up and reordered.

Can you put it back together correctly?

32: Hit the target

An instructor at a shooting range sets you a test. Three pistols are placed in front of you. Gun A, has a bias to shoot right, gun B shoots straight and gun C a tendency to shoot left. There is a silhouette of a figure moving around behind a blind that is programmed to respond to your shots in the same way a real person would.

What is the best sequence to fire the guns in so that you can be certain you hit the target?

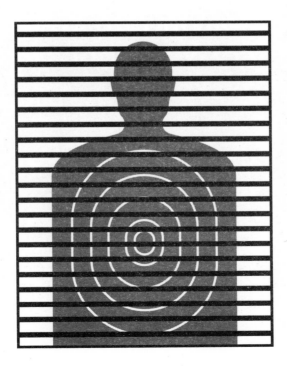

33: Decode the microdot

You find a message concealed in a microdot.

The only thing you know about the message is that it concerns a meeting and might have something to do with a local aerodrome.

NY XYD QY DY
KOBYNBYWO. QY DY
COMYXN WOODSXQ
ZYSXD

GKSD PYB PEBDROB
GYBN.

Using a simple Caesar substitution cypher, decode the message.

34: Computer access

You need the seven digit key code to open a restricted door. You suspect the code might be a date, but have no idea what it could be.

You contact a technical support agent to see if they can find out the code.

Minutes later they send you this:

1 0 0 1 0 0 0

You inform them that can't be the code because there's no 0 on the pad.

They then send you this:

1 0 / 1 / 0 /

You tell them that this can't be it either as it has slashes, and also has 0.

The tech support agent tells you they're sorry for any confusion, and that the code is actually both.

What is the seven digit code?

The Special Operations Executive

In 1940 the Special Operations Executive (SOE) was formed to support actions against the Nazi war machine behind enemy lines. According to Hugh Dalton, the Minister of Economic Warfare and in charge of the SOE, they were to specialize in "industrial and military sabotage, labour agitation and strikes, continuous propaganda, terrorist attacks against traitors and German leaders, boycotts and riots". At the same time, they were also tasked with creating underground armies in occupied territories that would rise up if Allied troops arrived. Such operations were extremely risky so training agents to undertake these dangerous but vital missions, often supported by local resistance groups, became paramount. Field agents were trained as commandos learning armed and unarmed combat. They had to be able to parachute, be skilled in demolition using explosives, to understand the use of radio equipment and Morse Code. Radio was the main form of communication using cyphers and codes to make sure the enemy were kept in the dark.

Members of the SOE were extremely varied, and included many women ranging from aristocrats such as Countess Krystyna, who saved two SOE agents from execution a few hours before they were due to die in a German prison and Noor Inayat Khan, the first female wireless operator to be sent to occupied France, to former Land Girl Violette Szabo; there were even individuals with criminal pasts. The SOE pioneered many successful missions, including Operation Jedburgh, in which more

SOE operatives wait to be secretly parachuted into France as part of Operation Jedburgh.

than 100 personnel and 6,000 tons of military stores were dropped into occupied France, making a vital contribution to the success of D Day in June 1944.

3

PART THREE

In the field

In the Field

In this final section you will be given a set of scenarios
that will test your skills as a spy. These range from
locating the hidden microdot, creating the best cover
story and discovering concealed bugs, to finding a
safehouse, uncovering the defector and cracking
fiendish codes.

   Secret agents often find that skills they can employ
in the abstract or in controlled situations become much
more difficult to use when in the real world. Sometimes
high-pressure situations mean that they don't have the
time or concentration to crack a code or assess someone's
actions. Other times it could be that they just don't have
the equipment they need or are in the wrong place at the
wrong time. Learning to stay calm and objective is
essential. But so is being able to make quick decisions,
as hesitation could lead to operational difficulties or even
a risk of being discovered. Being able to tell whether to

----

abandon an operation is one of the most difficult choices, and therefore extensively roleplaying such scenarios can give insight into those decisions.

It's also important to know how to exploit advantages. Sidney Reilly, the Russian-born agent later mythologized as the "Ace of Spies", was undercover in a German munitions plant in the build-up to the First World War. He wanted to get access to weapon schematics but had no idea of the plant's layout. He was working as a welder but volunteered to join the plant's fire brigade, which enabled him to convince the foreman to show him plans of the entire building showing the positions of hydrants and extinguishers, allowing Reilly to locate the weapon plans.

The puzzles in this section will be the ultimate test of all the skills you have developed during the course of this book.

35: Dead drop

A dead drop is a useful way to leave and receive messages
and items from another agent without exposing your
connection.

You must choose a dead drop from the marked locations on this normal suburban street, but it must be:

- Easily accessible by you
- Unlikely to be discovered by others
- Can be used without others finding it unusual.

Which location do you choose?

36: Fingerprints

A secret formula has been stolen from a government facility. You suspect one of the facility's scientists, Dr Anton Arnault. A partial fingerprint was located at the scene, but it doesn't match Arnault's prints kept on file. However, you suspect the file has been tampered with. Gloves are standard at the facility, so the only place you can obtain his actual fingerprints is from a surface in his house.

This is a report of the activity in his house just before you secretly enter at 8pm.

- 7pm: Usual cleaner leaves house. All surfaces wiped, no fingerprints present. Mrs Arnault (MA) still inside.
- 7:45pm: MA prepares dry martini, leaves it on counter.
- 7:50pm: Dr Arnault (DA) enters house from the cold exterior. Puts gloves in coat pocket, opens closet and hangs coat inside.
- 7:51pm: DA gives voice command to call colleague on video phone.
- 7:53pm: DA gives voice command to end call. Walks to laboratory counter in corner of room. Puts on surgical gloves.
- 7:55pm: DA examines unidentified material. Removes surgical gloves, throws into fire.
- 7:57pm: DA Goes to closet and opens it, removes coat and puts it on, puts gloves on and leaves house.

What is the one surface in the house that bears Dr Arnault's fingerprints?

37: You have been poisoned

You're in a bar monitoring a possible new contact. You finish your drink when you detect a subtle, yet bitter aftertaste.

You notice the bartender is leaving rather rapidly, removing his apron with haste. You realize you have been poisoned by an enemy agent!

The poison is probably quite fast acting and the drink is already making its way down your gullet. Should it enter your bloodstream it might be too late to apply any kind of antidote, even if you had one...

Looking at the objects in front of you, which two will be most effective at saving your life?

A-Glass of water

B-Salt shaker

C-Toothpicks

D-Slice of lime

E-Bowl of sugar

38: Strange disguise

A fellow agent has arranged to meet a contact and hand over a top-secret document to his handler. He is staying at a hotel and realizes that the lobby where they have agreed to meet for the handover will be busy and possibly full of enemy security agents who will be ready to pounce at any sign of the file being handed over, so the agent has secreted it in the hotel lobby. They can't get a message to their handler so they quickly decide to wear a visual clue from their wardrobe which will give the contact the location of the document.

Where is the document hidden?

39: Secret code

You need to gain access to a secret club, Club 5, often frequented by the enemy.

People in a group ahead of you take turns to speak code words to the doorman. The first says "A large bird of prey with huge wings and a hooked beak," and is admitted.

The second says "An animal caught and killed by another for food," and is admitted.

The third says "Wilfully deprived of all life by the actions of another," and is admitted.

The fourth says "The condition that differentiates plants and animals from non-organic matter," and is admitted.

What code words should you say to gain entry?

40: Title code

You are meeting with a librarian who you have convinced to hand over materials from a secret archive.

When you arrive, you start to think this might be a trap. When you see the librarian she (/he) hands you a piece of paper, but it's not the materials you expected but a list of books someone has checked out.

You suspect this is an enciphered message to you as the book codes don't match those in the library.

Looking at the codes you can tell that the first one, T14, is the letter L.

BOOKS CHECKED OUT:

T+14-The Use of Concealed Weapons

B+5- An Abridged History of Espionage

C+5-How The Cold War Ended and Why

L+9- Asymmetrical Warfare, a Very Simple Guide

C+3- A Code-breaker's Guide to Simple Ciphers

What is the one-word message the librarian is trying to give you?

41: Hidden microdot

An agent needs to pass a microdot of covert information to you. However, they are minutes away from being captured by enemy agents and the only means they have to pass it to you is three letters that are in their possession. They are able to leave them for you just before they are taken away.

Using only the visual information available, which letter has the microdot, and where?

Horace Fields
13 Lancaster Lane
Birmingham
B1 2RT

Dorian Tate
The Meadows
44–46 Buckingham Drive
Hampshire
BH23 8EP

Donninghan's Carpet Cleaning
Unit 8
Morpeth Business Centre
Northumberland
CA6 9PG

42: Checking for bugs

You return to your hotel to find there are signs that the enemy has planted some surveillance devices in your room.

By looking at photographs taken of the room before and after, can you tell where the six devices have been hidden?

1) _____

2) _____

3) _____

4) _____

5) _____

6) _____

The KGB and the Stasi

Spying is not just about gathering classified information from other enemy countries; having data about citizens in your own country can also be vital.

This was particularly important after the Second World War, when the Soviet Union established their own regime in Eastern Germany when the country was divided following the defeat of the Third Reich. West Germany was occupied by the Allies of Great Britain, the USA and France, and East Germany was occupied by the Soviets. More importantly, the strategic capital Berlin was also divided even though it was located in East Germany.

These events marked the beginning of the Cold War between the Western Bloc, led by the United States, and the Eastern Bloc, led by the Soviet Union and its Communist Party. The USSR's Intelligence service, the KGB, was given the responsibility of managing security in the Eastern part of Germany. The regime in Moscow soon realized that this was not a practical solution to making sure their strict policies were adhered to, however.

The Soviets decided that the best people to do this were the locals, and in 1950 they established the Ministry for State Security commonly known as the Stasi, to implement the principles of Communism. It was a mirror image of the KGB with their function to be the "Shield and Sword of the Party". From their headquarters in East Berlin, they exacted control of the rest of what was now called the German Democratic Republic (or GDR) by organizing a network of civilian informants to spy on friends, families and neighbours. By the end of the Stasi's existence in 1990 it had contributed to the arrest of approximately 250,000 people in East Germany.

The Stasi's duties were not just confined to suppression of the citizens; aided and abetted by the KGB, they indulged in espionage across Europe and the rest of the Western World.

A sign in front of the Brandenburg Gate in East Berlin warns visitors they are about to leave the Western section of the city.

43: Identify the target

You are pursuing two enemy agents.

 You need to be able to tell them apart, and know that the most dangerous one wears a distinctive red suit, while the other wears a blue one

 The only photograph you have of them is in black and white so you're unsure which of them is wearing a red suit, and which the blue.

Can you tell which agent is which?

44: Secret entrance

You enter a bookshop that you know has a secret entrance to headquarters. You need to pull out a specific book.

Many of the books have two things in common, but only one book, the one you must pull, has all three things in common.

Which is it?

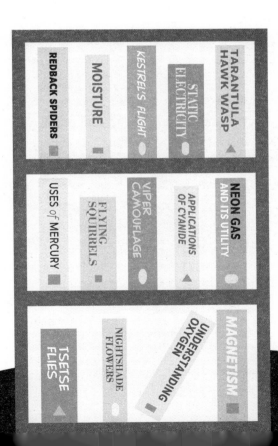

45: Surveillance

Here is a surveillance report by an agent who has been stationed in a house opposite a hotel. It is a possible hub of counter-intelligence activity, especially due to loading docks which have flat-bed trucks coming in and out all day.

Arrived at window and began surveillance.
Remained in apartment at window for entire shift.

4am-7:34am: Began shift. No activity.

7:35am: Young woman and older man enter building through main entrance.

7:36am-9:12am: No activity.

9:13am- 9:23am: Truck parked directly in front of hotel for 10 minutes, then drives into dock through gates.

9:23am-10:02am: No activity.

10:03am: Previous older man leaves via main entrance.

10:04-10:24am: No activity.

10:25am: Three men in staff uniforms enter via staff entrance.

10:25-11:59: No activity.

12pm: Finished shift.

The agent insisted they had accounted for everyone who had entered or exited the hotel via the front. But surely during the 10 minutes the truck was parked in front of the hotel, any number of individuals could have entered or exited without the agent seeing?

Assuming everything in the report is true, why is the agent correct?

a) They aren't, the agent is lying.
b) Because the truck was not parked in front of the hotel.
c) Because the truck did not obscure the agent's vision.
d) Because the truck was parked for less than 10 minutes.
e) Because it wasn't a truck.

46: Cover story

You are tasked with breaking into a military facility. On your way out you cut your hand quite badly on barbed wire.

When you arrive back at your hotel you find security forces waiting for you as they suspect your involvement. Your cover story is that you are a high-powered IT executive, who has been sent to your company's branch in this country to work remotely on a new system. You have been staying at the best hotel in town and living extravagantly on expenses, while lower level staff members run around doing your bidding.

Out of the following explanations, which is the best lie to tell to explain your injury?

1. You were using a screwdriver to fix a modem, and it slipped.
2. You were shucking an oyster at dinner and cut yourself on the shell.
3. You were unpacking some new equipment and cut it on the box cutter you were using.
4. You were trying to open a soup can for your supper.

47: The black vase

One of your assets requires regular visits, but it's not always safe to come to their apartment unobserved as they live in an area with many bars and cafes that's as brightly lit at night as it is during the day due to the many neon signs, including the Red Cat Cabaret directly opposite.

For this reason you have a code: if there is a red vase in the window, it is safe to visit, but if there is a blue vase, they are under surveillance.

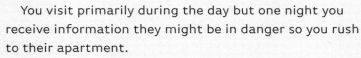

You visit primarily during the day but one night you receive information they might be in danger so you rush to their apartment.

You look in the window. The light is off in their apartment and there seems to be a black vase there.

What do you do?

1. Enter the building, they have put a black vase to indicate they're in danger but not under surveillance.
2. Enter the building, it's actually a red vase.
3. Don't enter the building, it's actually a blue vase.
4. Don't enter the building, an enemy agent has killed them and put a black vase there to taunt you.

48: Find the thief

A secret file has been stolen from an archive. It must have happened when someone was alone inside. Here are the suspect's statements.

Anton: I arrived at 8:55am and passed through the Lobby, unlocking everything and entering the Archive at 9am with Barbara. I stayed there until 12:30pm when I went to the Kitchen for lunch. I used the toilet at 12:53pm for about 4 minutes then resumed lunch, before returning to the Archive until 6pm when I left with Barbara and we locked up.

Barbara: I got there with Anton at five to nine and entered the Archive with him. I stayed in the Archive all morning, except I used the loo at five past ten for about twenty minutes. I had to leave at ten to twelve as I had a doctor's appointment, but I came back at half past two, and I worked until six when I left with Anton.

Carla: Arrived late due to traffic, entered the Lobby at 9:20 but had to tidy up a bit and entered the Archive at 9:30. Worked until 12:30 and then had my lunch break with Anton until 12:48 when I went back to the Archive. I stayed in the Archive until 5 when I went to pack up the van with Dieter and then left to try to beat the traffic.

Dieter: I arrived early for my half-day shift at 12:55pm, entered the Archive. Worked until 3pm and took a half-hour break, then went back to the Archive until 5pm, when I left with Carla to help pack up the van outside.

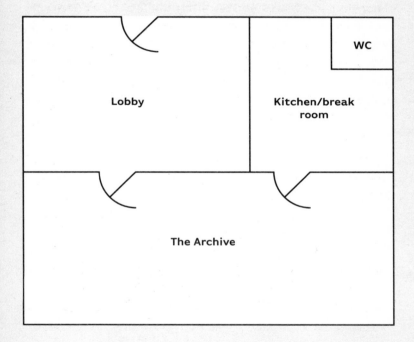

Which one of them stole the file?

Double Agents

Being a double agent is probably the most hazardous choice any intelligence officer can make. Whatever the motivation, whether it's ideological, political or monetary, spying for both sides is a dangerous game.

One of the most successful exponents of playing both sides against each other was Eddie Chapman, a small-time British criminal who became an agent for the German Abwehr Intelligence service and then MI5 at the same time. Chapman's confidence and amoral attitude convinced the Germans that he could be a valuable agent and he was trained in parachuting, explosives and radio communication in France before being parachuted into Britain to carry out a sabotage mission on an aircraft factory in Hatfield. Chapman, however, had other plans. Immediately on landing he surrendered himself to the police and was then taken to MI5, where he promptly offered his services to British Intelligence as a double agent. They helped him concoct a cunning piece of subterfuge where they disguised parts of the De Havilland aircraft factory he'd been sent to sabotage to look like he'd successfully damaged it, even planting a fake story in the *Daily Express* newspaper. His cover story was so convincing that on his return, he was asked to teach other German spies at an espionage school in Oslo while still passing secrets back to MI5. His incredible journey didn't stop there, Eddie Chapman was inducted into the German army as an officer and, even more astonishingly, awarded the Iron Cross, the highest German military honour.

In the 1950s and 60s Eddie Chapman sold the stories of his past exploits to publishers and newspapers, despite facing fines and government resistance.

49: Roulette

You're at the casino with a chip containing secret documents. You're told to bet it when the wheel shows 30 red.

Your contact informs you that the wheel's control mechanism is malfunctioning. They can't choose the number but they can tell you:

- The next number after a red will be black, unless it is odd, in which case it will be red again.
- The next number after a black will be red.
- The next number after an odd will be even, unless it is a prime number, in which case it will be odd again.
- The next number after an even will be odd.
- The next number after a double digit will be single, unless it has two of the same digit, in which case it will be double again.
- The next number after a single will be double.

If the most recent number is 33 black, what is the minimum number of spins you will have to wait before 30 red is possible?

50: Hair trap

You are undercover in another country. You cover was blown and you are being pursued by the authorities. To evade detection you are disguising yourself, keeping a low profile and using your skills to stay undetected. You have been wearing unobtrusive clothes with sunglasses and bleached your naturally black hair to blonde. However it's starting to wear off and you need to buy more peroxide to cover your roots.

As you leave your hotel room you are concerned it might be searched in your absence, so after you lock it you take one of your hairs and stick one end of it on the left side of the door crack, and the other on the right.

At the shop you are briefly concerned that the cashier has recognized you so you quickly take your leave.

When you return to your hotel room, you realize someone has been inside. The hair is there, and whoever entered your room has reapplied it in the same location as before, but there is something about the way they did it that made you realize their deception...

How can you tell someone was there?

51: Quick thinking

You have been undercover as a parking attendant at the underground car park of a block of luxury apartments. You are in contact with another agent who stays in one of the apartments pretending to be a pianist.

The residents normally leave their keys with you after they have parked, just in case you need to move their car for any reason.

You have just finished washing your fellow agent's car in the valeting bay and go to empty your bucket of dirty water down the nearby drain. You return to the car with a chamois leather and some wax, but notice a suspicious looking wire sticking out from underneath the bumper. You suspect an explosive device has been planted on the vehicle! Before you can act the agent arrives and asks for the keys to their car.

You must ensure they don't get in the car, but you suspect you are being observed, so you can't do anything suspicious or that would make people think you are connected.

What is your best course of action?

a) "Accidentally" drop the keys down the drain.
b) Hit him in the face with the chamois leather.
c) Lean over and whisper in his ear.
d) Take his arm and tap out a message in Morse Code.
e) Insist the car isn't ready and he must leave.
f) Attempt to remove the device yourself.

52: Find the key

An enemy's secret underground base has proved inaccessible because of the use of a special key. You manage to get hold of three keys, any of which might be the correct one, but you know if you use the wrong one they will be alerted.

The only information you have to tell which is the correct key is an end-on photo of it, taken with a miniature camera when it was resting on a desk.

Using this picture, can you tell which is the right key?

View of key from end.

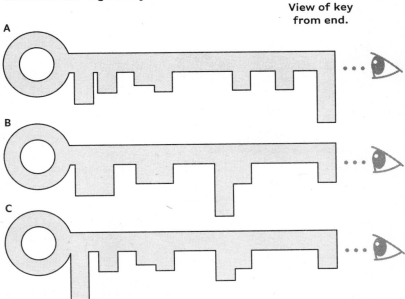

53: Spot the bug

You are sent to an embassy in a hostile country to check for listening devices. The embassy has recently undergone a refurbishment and deep clean by local trades people. During this process the coats of arms that adorned the walls of many of the rooms had been taken away for more intensive cleaning and then returned to their original positions. You are worried they could have been tampered with. The coats of arms should all be in pairs but something is not quite right.

Which two coats of arms have no match?

A

B

54: Observation

The secret three-word code is hidden right in front of you.

What is it?

55: Pick the cover

You're required to perform surveillance of Barcelona's Playa de La Barceloneta, in mid-December. Operating without local sanction. You need to choose an occupation or hobby for your cover identity that allows you mobility and an excuse to frequently be on the beach without being noticeable or challenged by authority.

A - Deckchair attendant
B - Fish and chip stall operator
C - Sea turtle spotter
D - Professional dog walker
E - Drug dealer

Which option should you choose?

56: Dead defector

You are assigned to help secretly move a defecting scientist from enemy territory across the border into a neutral country. Several options are discussed: That he is given a cover identity and false papers; that he uses a route and connections he already knows through his father to get to the border, and secretly notify you of the rendezvous point, or that he passes through a checkpoint hidden or disguised somehow.

Ultimately, you decide on an ambitious gambit: he will be in a coffin, supposedly dead! An injection of a drug to slow his heartbeat and some theatrical makeup will maintain the illusion.

You make all the arrangements, including bribing the coroner and having undercover contacts at the funeral parlour.

You wait at the checkpoint for the coffin to come through.

An hour passes and still no sign, but then a coffin arrives. A border guard insists that the coffin is opened. Once it's open he looks at the evidently alive defector and with a smile waves him past.

Why did the border guard wave the defector's coffin past?

57: Flip a coin

Microfilm can be concealed
in special hollow coins.

You have nine coins, six
of which contain secret
materials. Your only clue
to which six coins is this
composite image.

Which of the coins below contain the microfilm?

A   B   C

D   E   F

G   H   I

58: Sight line

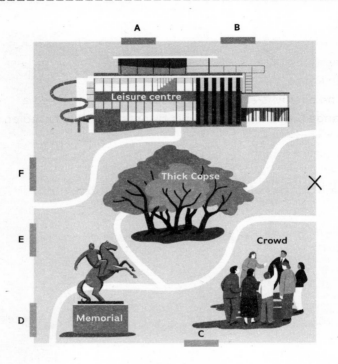

An agent has selected a vantage point from which to monitor a package (marked by X) that has been left in a rubbish bin so that she can identify the enemy agent who comes to collect it. She had the choice of six lower ground windows but there are various obstacles blocking the line of sight, especially after an elderly gentleman sitting on the bench collapses and a crowd gathers around him.

Using the position of these obstacles, which window did the agent decide to observe from?

59: Target pattern

You are on the trail of an enemy agent who is exposing spies across the world. You know all his targets, but you have limited resources and cannot protect them all.

The enemy is eccentric and seems to have picked a strange pattern to expose his targets, possibly based on their name.

3rd ~~SCOTT ARNHEIM~~
4th ~~BERTIE DAVIDSON~~
QUINCY DEVRIES
6th ~~SONNY FINCH~~
1st ~~PAMELA GIARDELLO~~
BRAD HITCHMAN
5th ~~GILLIAN MCINTYRE~~
STEPHEN SOAMES
2nd ~~ABBY VASQUEZ~~
DUNCAN WHITE

Can you predict who he will target next?

Crossing Borders

As you would imagine, travel as a secret agent is not without its challenges. Most of the time spies are not travelling under their given name, therefore providing them with fake documents that will withstand the most rigorous scrutiny from immigration officials or border guards is paramount.

During the Second World War, crossing borders by any conventional means was almost impossible for agents. Often they would be parachuted into occupied territory or arrive by submarine and then be taken ashore before making contact with local resistance organizations.

After the war Europe was supposed to be at peace, but the Cold War saw more challenges for the intelligence services on both sides of the Iron Curtain. Spies were often sent to a rival's country in the guise of a diplomat and given roles at the embassy that would allow them access to organizations or facilities. One example of this was David John Moore Cornwell (the real name of spy novelist John Le Carre) who was sent to Germany by his MI6 employers after the war. His cover was Second Secretary at the British Embassy in Bonn, and while there he could travel and carry out his duties under diplomatic protection.

Of course, frequently spies also have to smuggle information out of countries and various means of concealment have been developed. In one incident spies posing as Czechoslovakian priests helped to smuggle rolls of microfilm hidden in toothpaste tubes across the borders on the Ostend—Warsaw Express.

The border crossing at Helmstedt Marienborn in Germany.

60: Dry cleaning

You are being followed by enemy agents and need to do some "dry cleaning", the commonly accepted term for losing pursuers.

What is the best course of action in each of the options listed below?

1) You come to a café. Should you:
   a) Sit at a table and order a drink.
   b) Pass through the back entrance.
   c) Go to the toilet.

2) You come to a junction with a busy street and a quiet street. Do you:
   a) Go down the busy street.
   b) Go down the quiet street.
   c) Turn around and go the other way.

3) You get on a bus. Should you:
   a) Get off at the last stop.
   b) Get off at the next to last stop.
   c) Hide behind the driver.

4) You need to look behind to see how many people are still following. Should you:
   a) Turn around and look.
   b) Hold up a mirror.
   c) Go into a shop and use a mirrored surface.

5) You need to cross a road. Do you:
   a) Use an assigned crossing.
   b) Run across while cars are coming.
   c) Keep going until you can find an underground tunnel.

6) You come to a train station. Do you:
   a) Buy a ticket, get on a train.
   b) Buy a ticket, don't get on a train.
   c) Buy a ticket, get on a different train.

7) You think you have spotted a pursuer. Is it the person who is:
   a) Pointing at you.
   b) Idly examining a poster.
   c) Walking directly towards you.

8) You think you've lost them. Should you:
   a) Go directly to your safehouse.
   b) Never go to your safehouse again.
   c) Pretend to perform a dead drop.

61: Code words

An enemy agent has been converted into a double agent using compromising information. No one on your side has ever met them, but they have been reliably sending accurate information for months.

One day, however, the communication is terminated, and you begin to suspect the double agent has been discovered and that they could be in danger.

You want to preserve the asset and so using what information you have, you arrange for them to be extracted.

However, when you bring them into your safehouse, something seems off. You start to suspect that they are not the asset, but another agent impersonating them.

You gave the asset three code words to use to indicate their identity, but you are aware that if they had been captured, they might have revealed these details during interrogation.

The man you brought in, when asked, does give you the three code words.

But his response makes you certain he's a fraud.

If the double agent did in fact give the correct code words, how can you be so certain he's a fraud?

62: Listening device

You are undercover and have cultivated a close relationship with a foreign operative. You need to plant a listening device somewhere close to him in order to hear any communications he may have with his handlers. It's imperative that you clearly capture all his dialogue wherever he's located in the room. The device has a short range of one metre but is so small and light that wherever you plant it, he will not notice it.

His conversations are always on his encrypted satellite phone and he is inclined to move around the room while he is using it. There are a number of options, but you must choose the one location that has maximum efficacy.

Where is the best place to put the listening device?

63: One bullet

During a training scenario, you tasked with guarding a diplomat in a safe room high up in a block of flats. You leave the room briefly, and when you return find out that he has opened the curtains and is now being targeted by three people in the building opposite. They can all see him clearly in the well-lit room. You only have one bullet in your gun, and have to think fast.

Which shot should you take to save the target?

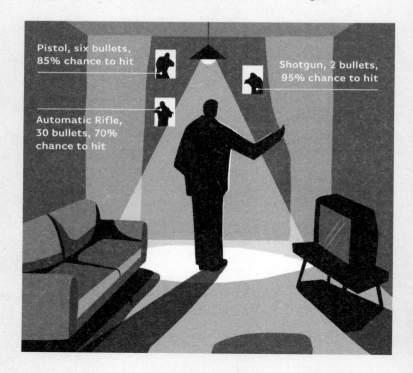

Pistol, six bullets, 85% chance to hit

Shotgun, 2 bullets, 95% chance to hit

Automatic Rifle, 30 bullets, 70% chance to hit

64: Micro message

You receive a cryptic note from a fellow agent who is embedded in a foreign power's security services. You have been tipped off that there is a microdot hidden somewhere in the text, but given no clue as to where it is. If you can find the dot, you will get the full message. The agent wouldn't have put it anywhere obvious.

Dear Gordon, further to our recent conversation I will put into action the plan for the new enhancement program as discussed. I'll get all the required clearances from our notable friends upstairs before I put any plans into practice, but that should be a formality. I am very optimistic that once you receive this message, everything will be clear so you will be able to see what I am saying, I will remain your devoted servant and colleague as always.

Michael

By using context clues within the message, can you work out where the microdot is hidden?

65: Track the tunnel

You have an idea of the entrance and
exit of an enemy escape tunnel, but
need to understand its path so you can
disrupt it without detection.

   The tunnel is not very deep
underground and cannot have been
dug through concrete, or anything
particularly tough. A photograph of
the area reveals several obstacles: a
shed with concrete foundations, a
pond, a thicket of trees, a deep well, a
dirt track, a statue, a stone obelisk
and an ornamental garden.

What is the path of the tunnel?

66: Sliding code

You are hacking a computer to learn a four-digit code.

The following image appears onscreen. You find that you can move the blocks in the direction of the arrow, and that they stop when they meet the line.

What is the four digit code?

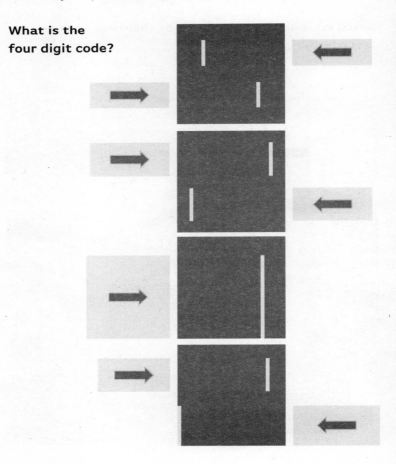

67: The wary agent

One of the people in this art gallery is a wary agent for your organization. They are very guarded against attack from enemy assailants and are very careful to ensure they can quickly exit any location.

Based on the following sketch of the room, can you identify the agent?

68: The house that wasn't there

You are given a map with instructions to meet another agent at a house. It says "Meet at 3 Northwood Road". That address does not seem to exist on the map.

Crack the encrypted instructions, and meet your contact at one of the designated secret locations marked on the grid with letters.

69: Scarface

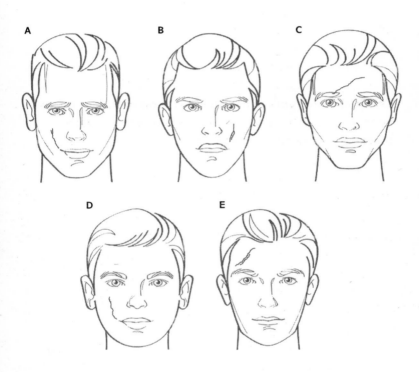

You only glimpsed the enemy agent for a moment when he passed behind you while you were standing at the bar in a hotel staring straight ahead. The agent was wearing a hat at the time but what marked him out was the scar on his left cheek. Back at HQ you are shown the following images.

Which one is the enemy agent?

70: The Silent Route

One Sunday you are instructed to take a blindfolded enemy agent from one part of town to a safe house in another. There are certain points along the route that have clearly audible clues which he might be able to hear and therefore work out his final location.

Looking at the map, what is the most viable path?

1. Church
2. The sea
3. Sports stadium
4. Emergency roadworks
5. Primary school
6. Train station

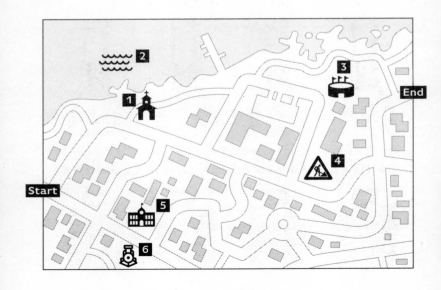

71: Vintage reds

The mission requires you to know your wine vintages, a familiar skill for any well-cultured operative.

You are to go to 20 Plaza Major, Madrid, where there's an establishment called Wines of Switzerland.

You will join a wine tasting session and meet an agent from an allied country. Picking the right vintage will connect you to your unknown colleague and alert them to their joint task, the downfall of a sinister organization at the heart of an oppressive regime. The only additional instruction you have been given is "Remember the house number, it's an important addition".

Which bottle should you choose?

Fact Turned Fiction

It will come as no surprise to fans of spy fiction novels, that many of the writers of this genre were once spies themselves. Roald Dahl worked for British Intelligence during the Second World War, and Graham Greene for MI6 as did Frederick Forsyth. It is even rumoured that Ernest Hemmingway worked for the KGB.

Ian Fleming, creator of the most famous fictional spy, James Bond, spent his time during the Second World War working for Naval Intelligence. He was a liaison for the navy to British secret government departments such as the Special Operations Executive (SOE), a precursor to modern day intelligence services. Through his role he was exposed to all the cunning schemes that were cooked up by these secretive organizations and the characters who populated these departments. This would fuel Fleming's James Bond novels and short stories and led to a multi-million-dollar film franchise.

David John Moore Cornwall, creator of enigmatic agent George Smiley, worked for both MI5 and MI6 in the 1950s and 1960s and was sent on covert missions across Europe. While still working for MI6 he started writing books, adopting the pseudonym John Le Carre as it was forbidden for Foreign Office staff to publish anything using their real names. His career in MI6 came to an end as a result of the exposure of British intelligence officers in Europe by the notorious double agent and traitor Kim Philby. He featured Philby as a KGB mole named "Gerald" in *Tinker Tailor Soldier Spy*, his most famous novel.

The impact Ian Fleming's creation James Bond had on real world espionage is widely disputed.

72: All flights lead to Rome

You're despatched to the airport to find a particular flight that arrives soon. You know that an international fugitive will be arriving, but don't know which flight they are on.

You have intercepted a series of numbers in an enemy communication, but they don't match the actual flight numbers of the planes.

The only clue you have is the phrase on the message, "When in Rome, count as the Romans count..." and the knowledge that 11-1000 is the Xiamen flight.

Flight Numbers

11-1000

1000-50

5-1-100

1-100-9

50-500- Fugitive's flight

"When in Rome, count as the Romans count..."

Can you match the departure cities with the numbers, and therefore work out which flight to intercept?

73: Video feed analysis

You are in charge of security at a secret facility. You begin to suspect that an enemy agent has entered the building. To cover their activities, the agent has hacked three of the security cameras to show previously recorded footage.

Using context clues, can you work out which three of the video screens have been hacked?

11 : 02

74: Synchronize watches

Five agents are given a mission which requires perfect timing to execute. They synchronize their watches to 22:08. One of them fails to meet at the rendezvous at the correct time, thereby jeopardizing the the entire mission.

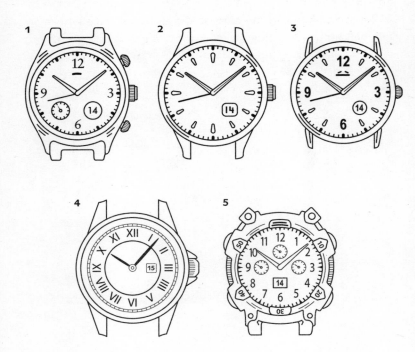

Which agent is out of synch?

75: Move the barrels

You are dropped into an enemy compound in order
to stealthily survey the set up.

   You have a limited amount of time to make your
observations before signalling for the helicopter to return
and pick you up

   You must make some sort of signal to indicate where
you will be for the pick up. You notices some barrels of
fuel that have been left in the shape of an arrow that is
pointing down to the right (A), however you will be waiting
on the left.

**How can you change the arrangement to (B)? The
barrels are heavy, so you have to move the minimum
amount as quickly as possible.**

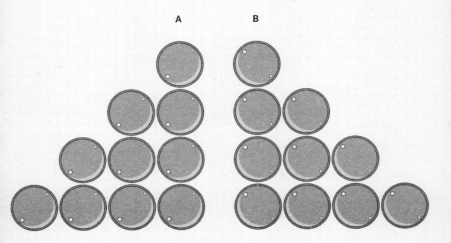

76: Detect the defector

A defector, known as a keen puzzle designer, insists that they will only allow someone of sufficient intellect to bring them in. You are told where and when to meet them but are given no description, only the following nonogram:

	13						2								13
						2	1	2	2	2					
			1			1	1	1	1	1			1		
		1	1	2	2	2	2	4	4	2	2	2	1	1	
		1	1	1	1	2	1	4	4	2	1	1	1	1	
		2	1	1	1	1	1	1	1	1	1	1	1	2	
	13	1	1	1	1	1	1	1	1	1	1	1	1	1	13
13															
1 9 1															
1 1 1 1															
2 7 2															
1 1 1 1															
1 1 3 1 1															
2 1 3 2															
2 5 2															
1 1 3 1 1															
1 1 1 1															
1 7 1															
1 1															
1 5 1															
1 1															
13															

Solve the nonogram and work out who is the defector.

77: Rendezvous

You are instructed to meet with a collaborator from an allied country. You receive a series of postcards of Paris landmarks and are told you must wait to recieve all five and then work out the rendezvous point.

Based on the images below,
where should you go?

78: Hidden message

You have to leave a message inside a book for a fellow
agent. You won't be present when they retrieve it and you
don't know anything about the agent, but they know that
somehow you'll make it clear which book they must open.

You only have enough time to touch four books, and you
can't remove any from the shelf.

What is the best way to hide the message?

79: Escape the room

You return to a room where an enemy agent has been imprisoned only to find that they have escaped.

However, you're not sure which of the possible escape routes they took. You know they didn't leave through the door you just opened as it has a security camera trained on it. As you enter the room you almost trip over a short step-ladder on the floor. The only other doorway is at the other side of the room with a black soot handprint on it. This is also monitored by a security camera.

From the light through the unopened skylight you can see a cupboard has been pulled open with a sooty handprint on the handle, a toolbox has been pulled out and opened with a hammer and screwdriver laying on the floor and four tiny screws.You can also see sooty handprints around an airvent with a metal grille on it.

The soot must have come from an open chimney which seems to have discharged black dust across half of the room, with a series of sooty footprints moving away from it.

Which escape route did the enemy agent take?

80: The barium meal technique

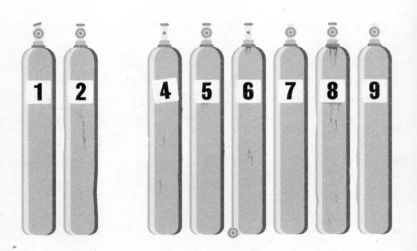

You suspect there is a mole in your organization. There are nine possible suspects.

You decide to use the "barium meal" technique to find out who is leaking information and will give a different, false piece of information to each of the suspects. You place nine canisters in the laboratory and you tell Suspect One that the first canister contains a special weaponized virus, Suspect Two that the second canister contains the virus, etc.

The next day you find the image above.

Which of the suspects is your mole?

81: Escape the cell

You have been imprisoned in a cell with no visible means of escape.

However, you have been informed that there is a deliberate weakness in one of the cell walls leading to a tunnel. You must strike one of the names written on the wall. But you haven't been told which, and must use visual clues to work it out.

Which name do you have to strike?

GEORGE

FRANK

RICHARD

ARTURO

XAVIER

82: Spot the disguise

An agent from a hostile nation is on the run, and headed for the airport where he is mingling with the other passengers. He has donned a very quick disguise to evade capture and hidden himself in plain sight.

How do you know which person of the three in front of you is the adversary?

83: Find the safehouse

You need to find a safehouse in a city, and have been given what appears to be a simplistic depiction of various building shapes.

But as you study the city's map you can't find buildings that correspond to this at all.

You then receive further information, telling you to go to the city's main road, but are not told which house to go to, only to "turn to the right".

The road is very long with almost 400 houses.

Which house number must you visit?

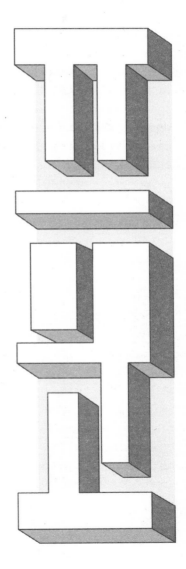

Spy Gadgets

Cars with ejector seats, exploding briefcases, a garotte wire concealed in a watch — all these gadgets have featured in spy movies but these kinds of devices are not just works of fiction. Some of the gadgets used by real spies are almost comical, like pigeons fitted with cameras, while others, such as cameras hidden in watches (first developed in the 1940s) are now commonplace. Many were and remain ingenious...

On 7 September 1978 Georgi Markov, a Bulgarian dissident living in London felt sharp pain in his thigh as he walked to work. He spotted a man behind him picking up an umbrella but thought nothing of it. When he got to work the pain was intense and he noticed a red spot on his leg. Four days later Markov was dead. Physicians were baffled but during the post mortem it was discovered that Markov had a tiny pellet measuring just 1.70 millimetres embedded in his leg. Analysis revealed the pellet contained a deadly toxin ricin. The subsequent investigation concluded that Markov was murdered by an agent of the Bulgarian Secret Service using the tip of the umbrella to deliver the poison pellet.

During the Cold War, devices for surveillance got even more ingenious, including a coat button camera which had a shutter hidden in the operative's pocket. Today, advances in technology are aiding agents with sophisticated pieces of equipment that are almost undetectable, including medical implants that can be hacked, microscopic listening devices and guns small enough to be concealed in a lipstick tube.

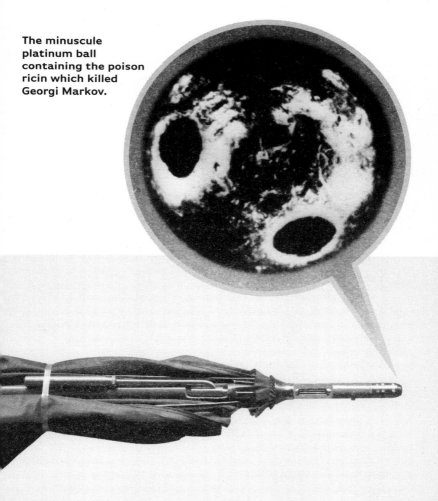

The minuscule platinum ball containing the poison ricin which killed Georgi Markov.

84: Unlock the box

You have broken into the house of a rich collaborator. They have an essential device kept in a special room, with extensive security measures that can only be deactivated by inputting the code number. The only clues you have to the code are a piece of paper you found tucked behind the box, and some paintings in the room in question.

On the back is written START FROM DOT.

1	4	2	2	2	2	2	i̇	4	3
3	1	4	1	3	3	3	3	2	1
4	1	4	2	2	2	2	1	3	4
2	2	4	3	3	3	3	1	1	4
2	4	2	2	2	2	4	1	4	2
1	2	4	3	3	3	3	3	1	1

What is the code number?

85: What day?

You receive a message from an asset you have placed within an enemy regime.

The spy wants a clandestine meeting at a specific time, at an exact location the following week. They even tell you what they will be wearing. But they have not included the actual day in the message.

How can you make sure you turn up a the right time in the right location for the rendezvous?

86: Choose your poison

You are meeting with two other people, one of whom you suspect might be an enemy agent. The waiter brings over three cocktails and you are concerned that one of them may be drugged.

Suddenly you get a message on your phone: two of the drinks are drugged!

If you refuse to drink the agent will be onto you.

But you have no way of telling which two of the three drinks are drugged.

In the end you decide to risk it and choose drink A.

Then, the agent picks up cocktail C and hands it to the third person in your group, who drinks it quickly. He then suddenly looks rather unwell and stumbles away. The enemy agent shrugs and waits for you to pick up your drink.

To give you the best odds of survival, should you stick with Cocktail A, or switch to Cocktail B?

87: Choose your equipment

You have a new mission to break into a secure facility which has no human guards in the grounds but instead has myriad other security measures. You must distract the guard dogs, deactivate the spotlights and then the cameras and gain entry through locked doors. You must do this quickly, without being identified, and need to photograph some files before destroying them. You must escape past the dogs again.

Which eight items should you select for your mission?

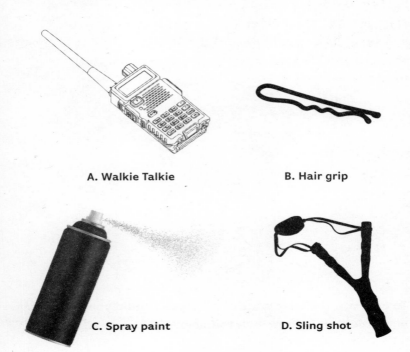

A. Walkie Talkie

B. Hair grip

C. Spray paint

D. Sling shot

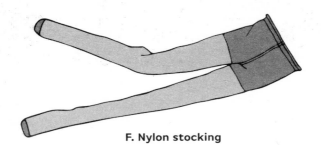

F. Nylon stocking

G. Beef steak

H. Stun Grenade

I. Micro camera

J. Matches

K. Machine gun

L. Tennis ball

88: Locate the facility

You are told that there is a covert facility you must travel to on the Isle of Man. You are told to plan a journey from Shoulaige-e-Caine to The Bungalow, then from The Bungalow to Onchan, then from Onchan to Crosby and finally from Crosby back to Shoulaige-e-Caine.

But before you can leave, you are contacted and told that the facility is in fact at none of those locations but that you have all of the information needed to find it's real location.

Using the map with the locations marked, where is the facility?

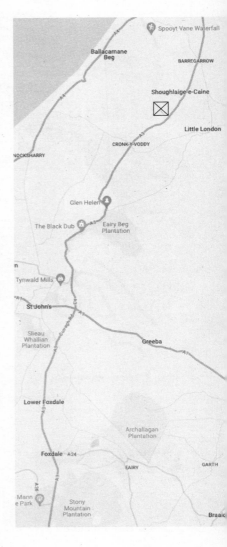

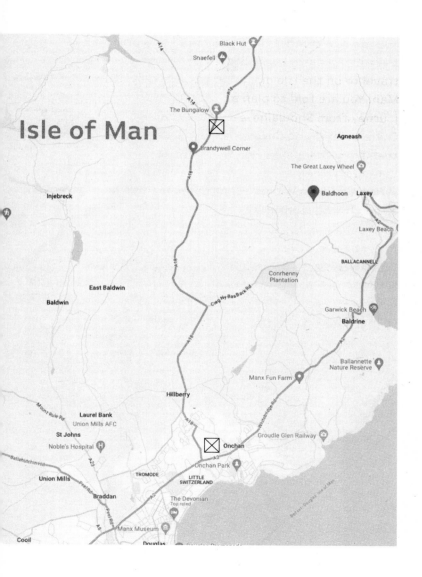

89: Where's Gratzki?

You are researching the background of a prominent
businessman who is suspected of being a spy. There were
rumours he had a connection to Gratski, a well-known spy
runner, but you cannot find any photos of them together.

However, you do find one photo that you think may have
been altered, and rather inexpertly, to remove someone,
possibly Gratski.

**What evidence is there that someone has been removed
from this photograph?**

90: Hack the phone

You urgently need some codes
contained on an enemy agent's
phone but unfortunately in the
tussle for the device, he is knocked
out cold.

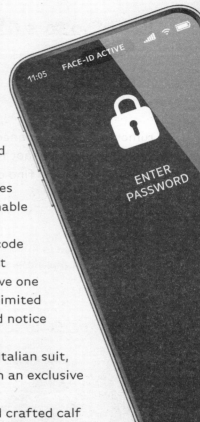

You know his phone has the codes
but as he's unconscious you are unable
to get his passcode to unlock the
phone. It's possible his ten letter code
may be based on some detail about
himself or his life. But you only have one
attempt to unlock the phone and limited
time. You look at him for clues and notice
the following:

- He's wearing an expensive silk Italian suit,
  bespoke by the looks of it, from an exclusive
  tailor in Rome.
- His shoes, also Italian, are hand crafted calf
  leather, but have a scuff on the left one.
- He has a full head of naturally greying hair but it's
  been dyed jet black, probably by him.
- He has a distinctive scar (dueling?) on the right cheek
  of his handsome face.
- He's sporting an expensive time piece on his left wrist.

**Using what you know and can observe, how do you
unlock the phone?**

91: Secret exit

You identify a secret hideout of an enemy agent and take a small group of your agents to apprehend them.

However, when you arrive there's no sign of them, the building in fact seems stripped of items and furniture. But as it was constantly being watched you can't understand how they escaped.

There's something odd about one of the rooms, though...

Where is the possible secret exit?

92: An enigma

For months the enemy has been using a particularly complex cipher. However, your team of cryptologists have finally managed to crack the code, and are able to read the enemy's messages.

One of the messages reveals that they intend to attack one of your power facilities that night.

You don't want the enemy to realize you have cracked the code, so consider the following options:

1. Evacuate power plant
2. Replace staff with agents, and apprehend saboteurs
3. Close power plant down
4. Reroute power from plant so it's non-essential
5. Send message to allies warning of plot

Which combination of actions should you take, or not?

The Art of Disguise

Infiltration without detection is vital to any successful spy network, which is why intelligence agencies have invested so much time and effort in perfecting this art.

Techniques can be as simple as altering a person's features. A good disguise is always additive; intelligence agencies can make someone taller, fatter or older, but it is difficult to go in the other direction. Agents might have a particular way of walking or talking, so might suddenly have a limp or a speech impediment, even placing an artificial palate in their mouths to maintain the façade. If they are trying to remain undetected on foreign soil, it is not enough to simply speak the language fluently, the agent must display local idiosyncrasies. These new habits need to become second nature because one slip could be deadly.

The ability to adopt a quick change of look can be key in shaking off a tail. A good agent will have access to small props, like a hat, glasses or reversible jacket, that can change a look and help them become temporarily invisible.

Becoming what intelligence agencies call "Sleepers" requires a whole new set of skills. These spies must literally become a part of a local community, known, trusted and inconspicuous all while they are carrying out their espionage duties. Or they maybe just be living and going about their daily lives until they are activated by their handlers. They can merge into society by procuring the birth certificates of long dead people and creating a new person with that name, even down to getting a passport so they can move freely back and forth without suspicion.

An overcautious spy trying to blend in needs to remember that often passersby are more concerned with their own appearance than theirs.

93: The capsule

A captured spy may be expected to make "the ultimate sacrifice". One of your agents has been captured and realizes the interrogator is a master of the field and they'd soon spill all their secrets. They have a capsule of quick-acting, yet undetectable poison. But before they can take it another captured agent is brought in. The second agent doesn't know as many secrets, but the ones they do know would be much more dangerous for the agency.

As the hot lights beam down and the interrogator taunts them by drinking his third glass of water in half an hour, your agent has to make a quick decision.

Who should consume the poison for the good of the agency?

94: Find the phrase

You are trapped in enemy territory and are told that some local truckers will be prepared to smuggle you out if you give them the right two-word phrase.

A fire that burns not yellow, or blue, but red, can be the start of a mighty inferno, if it is given the oxygen of freedom. And a white flame can, in the end, have no more effect on the world than a herring on the sea.

You've been given a passage torn from a book, and the advice "tenth word from the start, and fourth word before the end".

What is the passcode?

95: Exploiting fear

Your assignment is to get information from an enemy operative. They are known to be tough and impervious to just about every method of inducement, from truth serum to more "hands on" interrogation. Their only known weakness is severe arachnophobia!

The plan is to smuggle a spider into their hotel room. The quartermaster offers you a choice of eight-legged creatures.

Which one is the right beast for the job?

Tarantula (*Theraphosidae*): Venomous, the largest arachnid family on the planet.

Black Widow (*Latrodectus*): Highly venomous their bite has been known to cause death to humans.

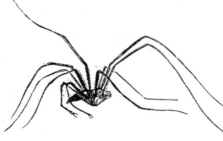

Harvestman (*Opiliones*): Otherwise named Daddy Long Legs, emits an odour when threatened.

Brown Recluse (*Loxosceles reclusa*): has tissue-destroying venom.

Brazilian Wandering Spider (*Phoneutria*): Its bite can lead to paralysis then death.

Funnel Web (*Hadronyche*): Extremely venomous and highly aggressive.

96: Message on a bottle

A secret message from your handler will be placed inside a seemingly innocuous bottle of BBQ sauce concealed on the shelves of a local supermarket. You'll have to act quickly.

Which bottle looks different and therefore contains the secret message?

97: The mole

You are called to the office of your superior. He says he was tasked with finding a double-agent in the organization.

He says he has discovered it's you.

"I released secret information to each of the suspected agents. You, Heidecker, Finnian, Nadal. The piece of information I gave you was immediately leaked. I didn't want to believe it so I did it again, several times. And each time the enemy got hold of the information. None of the other agents were given the information I gave you, although Heidecker seemed to have an inkling about one of them. So you must be the double-agent."

You know that it's true that the information you were given ended up in the hands of the enemy. But you also know you're not the mole.

Logically, who must be the mole?

98: Hornet drone

You must input the right set of instructions to make this hornet drone travel through the air vents. However, the system has crashed and now the inputs have been replaced by symbols. You know the three instructions are Forward, Turn Left and Turn Right.

All that you know is that the first drone you sent crashed in the place marked when you gave it the following instructions:

◉x7 ❖ ◉x2 ■ ◉x3 ❖ ◉x2 ◉x2 ❖ ◉x3

Which of the following input chains will get you to the destination?

A) ◉x6 ■ ◉x2 ❖ ◉x2 ❖ ◉x3 ❖ ◉x3 ■ ◉x4

B) ■ ◉x2 ❖ ◉x2 ◉x3 ❖ ◉x3 ■ ❖ ◉x4 ◉x6

C) ◉x7 ■ ◉x2 ■ ◉x4 ❖ ◉x2 ■ ◉x3 ❖ ◉x3

D) ◉x7 ❖ ◉x2 ■ ◉x4 ■ ◉x2 ◉x3 ❖ ❖ ◉x3

Start

Finish

99: The cipher scenario

Stationed in Geneva, near the Rue Du Stand, you're told to expect an encrypted message with the time and location of your next rendezvous with your handler.

You receive a spam email and identify the encoded message within it:

QY JE PYPDUUX HKO TE CJQDN DGE ZW

However, you have been given two different fixed codewheels, and do not know which to use to decipher the message: **A** or **B**?

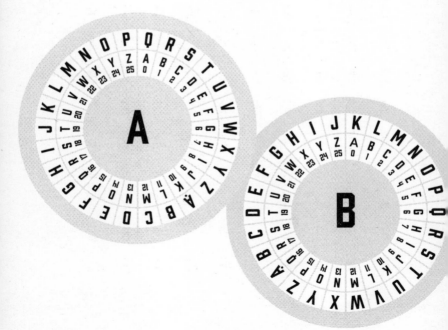

Time is of the essence, so you leave a copy of the day's newspaper in your dead drop to signal that you need help. Hours later, you find a single note tucked inside it. Remembering your training, you carefully treat the paper with a special chemical, and a grid of **A**s and **B**s is revealed...

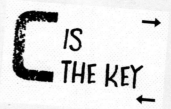

Use these details to decode the message.

B	B	B	A	A	A	B	A	A	→
A	A	B	A	B	B	A	A	A	B
A	B	B	A	B	B	B	A	B	A
B	A	B	B	A	A	A	A	A	B
A	B	B	B	B	A	B	B	B	B
B	B	A	B	A	A	B	A	A	A
B	B	A	A	B	A	B	A	B	B
A	A	A	B	A	A	A	A	B	A
B	B	B	A	B	B	B	A	B	B
B	A	A	B	A	B	B	A	A	←

100: Orienteering

You have already arranged to meet your handler at the Guggenheim in Manhattan at 4pm. So you are confused when you receive a map that seems to show a completely different, more remote location in an entirely different country.

Furthermore, you know for a fact that Lake Bordon is heavily polluted and would not be a suitable place to meet, even in a boat. But then you start to suspect your handler may have been telling you something else...

Where and when should you meet your handler?

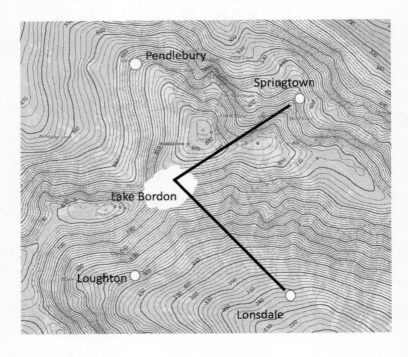

101: Cryptography

For your final test you must decode the following passage.
You know it is a Vigenère cypher so every letter will be
encoded differently according to a code phrase but you
haven't been given the phrase. All you know is that it
appears on almost half the pages of this book.

What is the encoded message?

MOMK XQ
MLW XGK
SX IFX
XWLM

Traitors and Defectors

Every country has had their own famous traitors, double agents who are persuaded to work for the enemy for a variety of reasons – ideological, political, because of blackmail or simply because they are paid a lot of money.

Arguably the United Kingdom's most renowned example is the Cambridge Five, Donald Maclean, Guy Burgess, Kim Philby, Anthony Blunt and John Cairncross. Recruited by the then Soviet Intelligence Service, the NKVD, during their time at Cambridge University in the 1930s, the motivation for this ring of spies was ideological as they believed that Soviet Communism would prove to be best defence against the menace of Fascism that was on the rise in Germany. After university, the spies took up roles at the very heart of British intelligence, including at the Foreign Office and MI6. Blunt was even the Surveyor of the King's (late the Queen's) Pictures from 1945–1972. In total they passed over 17,000 secret documents to the Soviets. Remarkably all of them escaped prosecution by either defecting to the Soviet Union (Burgess, Maclean and Philby) or confessing in return for immunity (Blunt and Cairncross).

In the US, there were a number of spies secretly working for the Soviet Union during the Cold War, including FBI agent Robert Hanssen, CIA counterintelligence officer Aldrich Ames, naval officer John Anthony Walker, and Julius and Ethel Rosenberg.

One of the Cambridge Five, John Cairncross, in France in 1990

Julius and Ethel Rosenberg in the back of a police van following their conviction for espionage in 1951. Both were executed in 1953.

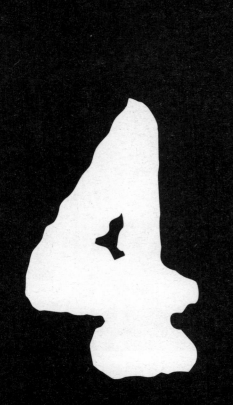

PART FOUR

Solutions

Solutions

1: The empty chairs
Once the nonogram is complete, only one chair is accessible along the path from the starting arrow: C.

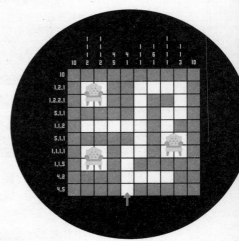

2: Advice column
The love rival didn't predict the number.

The letter writer said the love rival was surrounded by dozens of knick-knacks. It would have been easy for him to put a piece of paper with each possible number into a lot of different boxes, vases and so on, then remember which one had which number when the letter writer named it.

3: Pop up
The solution is 1D, 2A, 3C and 4B. Placing the mirrors in those locations will cause the laser to reflect at a 45-degree angle, spelling out the number 5.

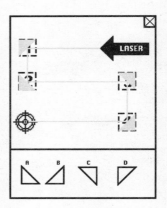

4: Job advertisement

The ten errors are:

1. The job is claimed to be both temporary and permanent.
2. It asks for outdoor workers for a clerical role.
3. It says the company is in Scotland when its address is in Wales.
4. Its hours are 9pm to 5:30am but the job is clearly not a night-time role.
5. The company's logo says MISJ but the address says MIJS.
6. It asks for over 15 years experience but then suggests young people can apply.
7. The pay is listed in dollars.
8. The pay is ridiculously high.
9. "Mongeese welcome" is a non-sequitur.
10. It claims the company makes paper but the address says it is a pharmaceutical company.

5: The hourglass riddle

The solution to the riddle is that the glassmaker should remove the stopper of the silo and wait for all the sand to drain out. As it is made from his special glass not a single grain will remain and then once it's all gone he can answer truthfully: zero grains of sand.

6: Join the dots

The clue indicates that you need to join the odd numbers together and then the even numbers. If you do this, you will make shape A.

7: Magazine advertisement

You add the current issue number to the width and subtract it from the length.
Issue 1 is 9 x 10
Issue 2 is 8 x 11 (9-1, 10+1)
Issue 3 is 6 x 13 (8-2, 11+2)
Issue 4 is 3 x 16 (6-3, 13+3)
This would make Issue 5 the impossible size of -1 x 20 (3-4, 16+4), hence the manufacturing problems.

8: Betting odds

You want a horse with "unique odds and a unique name". Amber Dragon, Sapphire Light, Marigold Dreamer, and Emerald Isle all basically have the same odds expressed different (5/1). Only Major Mustard and Scarlet Rose have unique odds.

But they are all colour based names, and Major Mustard shares a colour type with Marigold Dreamer (yellow) meaning Scarlet Rose (red) is the horse you want.

9: Spy movie poster

The clue of a "positive attitude" indicates you must choose the numbers that are in the parts of the tagline that have positive adjectives.

ONE *amazing* mission,
EIGHT *ingenious* assassins,
THREE terrifying hours,
FOUR *beautiful* women,
FIVE deadly warheads.

10: Doorbells

The Local Imports buzzer says to call JB. This could mean Jean Bertrand but you can't call her before 7pm or James Benton but you can't call him after 5pm, so that leaves Jane Burlington. The note on her bell says to ring the denist. Dr Arthur Heritage has DDS after his name, indicating he is a dentist, but says to ring GI after 6. This can't be Gareth Inskip because he no longer lives there, so you need to ring Gloria I Reynolds.

11: The Koan Card
If you connect "like to like" (1-1, 2-2 etc) it forms a forwards arrow.

There were **12** groups.

They were all animals of different species and manner.

13 Cats, **35** pigs, **64** dogs, **42** birds.

All equal in stature. If a man were to tell

57 lies and **76** truths

12: Crime prevention leaflet

Here's the location of the six observers. Spies avoid the obvious such as waiting in a car or hiding behind a newspaper.

- Shadow behind tree
- Using hand mirror
- Periscope
- In window
- Homeless man lying on the ground
- Pushing pram

13: Want to be a spy?
The border of the "ad" is actually Morse Code. It spells out "IF YOU ARE NOT A FOOL CONTACT PO BOX 59009D'

14: Letter to the editor
The misunderstanding is in point 3. As Dr Hanley is American he would naturally be referring to 85 Farenheit, which is 29 Celsius, uncomfortable for humans but still survivable.

15: Shop window cards

If you pick up on the clues, you should follow this path:

16: Number response

The 5 response numbers are the number of letters in each of the five number words. (One has 3 letters, two has 3, three has 5 etc). Therefore the correct response to "Six Five Eight Three Two" is d) 3 4 5 5 3.

17: Safe word

M=0 means that the alphabet is the key to the word code, with M at the centre. A-L are the 12 notches on the left and N-Z the 13 notches on the right. With that in mind N E V E R translates to turning the dial 1 to the right, 8 to the left, 9 to the right, 8 to the left and finally 5 to the right.

18: Keypad

Using logical deduction, this is the position of the numbers.

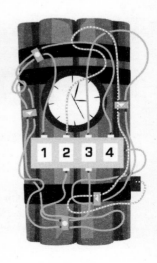

4	7	9
5	1	2
8	6	3

19: Defuse the bomb

CIRCLE indicates the wires go straight through, and TRIANGLE indicates they cross, otherwise line 1 would not be able to go through the junction at the bottom. Line 2 is the one you must cut.

20: Connected nodes

Once you have solved the
Sudoku, apply the connections
as shown on the numbers results
in only one unbroken path,
from B to G.

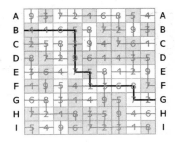

21: The hidden signal

The operation is launched on Day 6. The message is identical
every day, but the readers alternate between Mr and Mrs,
except for Day 6, when it is a man again.

22: Minefield

The solution is to find the
prime number sequence to get
across the mine field: 11, 3,73,
47,7,89,23, 71, 13,79 5,17,61.

99	11	28	42	1	66	15	50	36	25
27	49	3	26	45	6	62	14	58	34
74	73	8	46	18	68	12	56	75	22
10	40	47	19	21	48	9	63	16	15
100	64	30	7	82	23	71	20	44	77
76	39	52	98	89	60	91	13	84	38
25	90	57	4	32	65	51	33	79	93
94	35	85	54	80	78	17	5	81	72
70	88	24	92	96	61	86	95	69	87

23: Find the file

Each of the three information boxes on the page have a letter in
all four corners. The boxes also have one, two and three lines
respectively. The code matches these letter's positions, for
example the top left corner of the double-lined box is F

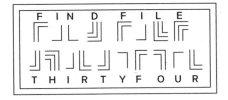

24: Frequency analysis
If you add Signal A to Signal C, the corresponding waves will cancel out enough of the amplitude to result in the target signal.

25: Find the micro cameras
These are the positions of the cameras, with camera D pointing at the mirror which is why the clock numbers are in reverse.

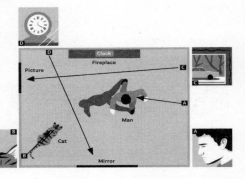

26: A suitable code
The ideal code is H0I8I0H, as it reads the same if flipped horizontally or vertically, whereas all the other numbers could be mistaken for different numbers if that happens.

27: Destination code wheel
At the top the code reads QZLSX.
If you count the quantity of each letter they equal:
Q=6   Z=7   L=14   S=10   X=11
If you use the cypher key 6, 7, 14, 10 and 11 translates to Delhi.

28: Anonymity
As you are unknown to the enemy agent, the quickest and most efficient thing to do is not to disguise yourself at all!

29: Take a shot
The winner is Agent C. Although it appears as if they have only used one shot, they have in fact fired 5 shots so accurately they have all hit the same mark.

30: Seat plan

The best seat is the one furthest to the front. The text says that the counter agent is experienced, so he will no doubt be looking for someone behind him. Since you are in an enclosed environment with no other exits, you can sit at the front and be sure he can't leave without you noticing. Sitting at the front also means you will have extra leg room and can easily move around anyone sitting next to you when the agent does make his move.

31: Sector assignment

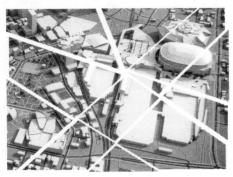

32: Hit the target

Pick up gun A and C in each hand and fire them simultaneously at the target, then fire gun B, as the target will move to the middle to avoid the other shots.

33: Decode the microdot

If you consider the message could concern the local aerodrome you might notice one of the words has the same number of letters as AERODROME (9). If you use that as a key, then you can work out the shift that the letters have taken:
Then decode the message as DO NOT GO TO AERODROME.
GO TO SECOND MEETING POINT WAIT FOR FURTHER WORD.

K=A	L=B	M=C	N=D	O=E	P=F	Q=G	R=H
S=I	T=J	U=K	V=L	W=M	X=N	Y=O	Z=P
A=Q	B=R	C=S	D=	E=U	F=V	G=W	H=X
I=Y	J=Z						

34: Computer access
The code is 1891989, shown by combining the two images.

35: Dead drop
The best possible location is the broken and rusted water fountain. The full litter-bin will no doubt be emptied at some point; the postbox will be locked, tampering with it would be noticed and it will also be emptied; the fusebox is also locked; and the manhole cover would lead to the sewers. The tree-hole might be a possibility, but a squirrel may interfere with any contents. The broken water fountain would be a good place to slip something small as no-one would try to drink from it and the rust implies it's unlikely to be repaired soon.

36: Fingerprints
He does not drink the cocktail, destroys the surgical gloves he wears when touching the material, only makes voice activated calls and is wearing gloves when he enters and leaves, so the only place his fingerprints are present would be the handle of the closet where he put his coat and gloves after he has taken them off.

37: You have been poisoned
The two objects you need are A) the water and B) the saltshaker. If you add a lot of salt to the water and then drink it, it will make you vomit, expelling the poisoned drink from your gullet as quickly as possible.

38: Strange disguise
The agent is wearing a flower, and also has mismatched black and white shoes, to indicate that the file is hidden behind the floral ying and yang on the wall behind him.

39: Secret code
After the first statement, each subsequent statement is the definition of the 5th word in the previous statement: Prey, Killed, and Life. To get in you should give a definition of the word "Plant", eg "A living organism such as a tree, flower or shrub that typically grows in the ground."

40: Title code
In the title of the first book, the letter L is 14 spaces from the first occurrence of the letter T. Following this pattern, 5 letters on from B is E, 5 letters on from C is A, 9 letters on from L is V and 3 letters on from C is E, spelling LEAVE.

41: Hidden microdot
The microdot is hidden on letter A, behind the stamp.

All of the letters have been postmarked after being sent, but on the first letter the mark cannot be seen on the stamp, indicating it has been applied after the fact and is where the microdot is hidden.

42: Checking for bugs
Here are the bug locations, indicated by:
1) Painting upside down
2) New power socket
3) Light fixture higher than before.
4) Book is now upright.
5) Photo frame now oval
6) Banana in fruit bowl.

43: Identify the target
The man on the left's suit is the same colour as the stop sign in the background, which is traditionally red, therefore he is the dangerous spy and the other man is the blue-suited one.

44: Secret entrance
The books' subjects fall roughly into three categories:
1) Things that are or can be airborne.
2) Things that cannot be seen.
3) Things that can be deadly.

The only thing that falls into all three categories is Neon Gas, being an invisible airborne gas that is deadly to humans if breathed.

45: Surveilance
The answer is c) because the truck did not obscure the agent's vision. The report mentions that the hotel is next to loading docks, which may necessitate the use of flat-bed trucks. If the flat-bed was empty the agent could see directly through to the hotel.

46: Cover story
The best response is 2, you were shucking an oyster from its shell. While you are working in IT you're an executive and therefore unlikely to be doing the manual work. And as you're dining extravagantly you're also unlikely to be opening a can.

47: The black vase
The correct answer is 3. Don't enter the building, it's actually a blue vase. It is your first time visiting at night, and blue objects under red light (such as the sign of the Red Cat Cabaret) appear to be black.

48: Find the thief
The thief must be Carla as she is the only one who had opportunity to be in the Archive on her own. When Anton went to the toilet Barbara had left, and Dieter had not arrived yet, giving her a very short window to sneak in and steal the file.

49: Roulette

If the most recent number is 33 Black, it's possible the NEXT spin could be 30 Red, because:

- The next number after a black will be red.
- The next number after an odd will be even, unless it is a prime number, in which case it will be odd again. 33 is not a prime number.
- The next number after a double digit will be single, unless it has two of the same digit, like 33, in which case it will be double again.

50: Hair trap

Your hair is blonde with black roots. You originally stuck it on with the black part on the left, but it now has the black part on the right.

51: Quick thinking

The best tactic is a), "Accidentally" drop the keys down the drain. If you hit him in the face with the chamois leather it will seem strangely hostile, and whispering in his ear or taking his arm will also seem suspicious. Insisting he leaves or trying to remove the device yourself will also draw too much attention.

Dropping the keys is suspicious but of the options available it is the most plausible.

52: Find the key

C is the correct key as it is the only one whose design matches how it appears in the picture from the front.

53: Spot the bug

C and F do not match, as the wings on the right-hand griffin in F are much larger than those in C.

54: Observation

The code is hidden in the running head of the page.

98   THE SPY THAT

54: Observation

- -

The secret three-word code is hidden right

What is

55: Pick the cover
The best cover identity is D. Professional dogwalker. Deckchairs would not be needed on the beach in December, Fish and chips are not commonly sold on the beach in Barcelona, Sea turtles come onto the beaches in Summer and Drug dealers, while common, would still possibly attract police attention.

56: Dead defector
The border guard let him pass because he's the border guard for the other side of the checkpoint, inside the country he's defecting to.

57: Flip a coin
The composite coin is made of the following coins:

58: Sight line
The only vantage point not blocked is C. The crowd block it now, but they were not there when the selection was made and will soon disperse.

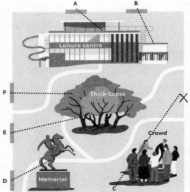

59: Target pattern
The agent is exposing his targets alphabetically, but based on the second letter of their names: PAMELA, ABBY, SCOTT, BERTIE, GILLIAN, SONNY. Therefore the next target will be BRAD HITCHMAN.

60: Dry cleaning
1) b This can be effective in obscuring your path.
2) a Busy streets will conceal you better.
3) b Getting off at the next to last stop will wrongfoot them.
4) c The other two options are too obtrusive.
5) a This will create the least attention.
6) b If you try to board a train with no ticket it will draw focus.
7) b Pursuers usually try to disguise their interest.
8) c You need to test if you are clear, pretending to do a dead drop will pique the interest of any remaining followers and cause them to pause and/or show themselves.

61: Code words
The supposed double-agent gave you the code words, but not in the correct order.

62: Listening device
The best place to plant the bug is on the foreign operative himself. The text says that you are undercover and have develoed a close personal relationship with him so you will have the opportunity. As it's such short range that is the only place where you could guarantee to hear everything said, and it's light enough that he won't notice.

63: One bullet
You should shoot the lightbulb, plunging the room into darkness, which would mean none of them would be able to target them, in just enough time to get them out of the room.

64: Micro message
The microdot is hidden as the apostophe in the "I'll" that begins the second sentence. The message does not use contractions except for that one place.

65: Track the tunnel
This is the only possible tunnel route.

66: Sliding code
If you slide the blocks to where the lines are, the numbers 5879 are formed.

67: The wary agent
The agent is person F. They are standing close to the door, with their back against the wall, offering them a quick escape without vulnerability to assassins.

68: The house that wasn't there
The clue indicates you have to move 3 grid spaces NORTH of WOOD ROAD. Therefore the secret location is B.

69: Scarface
It can't be C or E as their scars would not be visible if they were wearing a hat. The agent was glimpsed in a mirror, so their left side scar would actually be on the right side of their face. Therefore B is the enemy agent.

70: Silent route

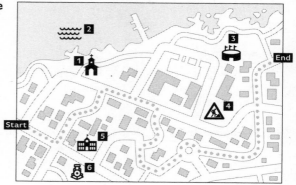

71: Vintage reds

The Swiss flag gives you the clue that you must add up all the numbers of each date.

1+9+6+6=22 1+9+7+3=20 1+9+7+5=22 1+9+8+4=22

1973 is the only one that adds up to 20, the house number of the bodega.

72: All flights lead to Rome

Each of the destinations contains Roman numerals in their name. The flight numbers are those numbers, e.g. XIAMEN is 11-1000.

The rest are:

SAINT CROIX 1-100-9

LONDON 50-500 (The fugitive's flight)

VENICE 5-1-100

MONTREAL 1000-50

73: Video feed analysis

The hacked screens are:

A It shows a clock with 3:55, when the time on the console is 11:02.

C It shows the man spilling coffee on himself, and the same man is on screen E with the coffee stain already there.

D The glass in the background is full with ice, but screen F show that the ice in the glass has melted.

74: Syncrochize watches

Watch 4 is the unsynchronized watch. Although it has the same time as the others, it says it's the 15th while the others say the 14th.

75: Move the barrels

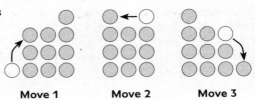

Move 1   Move 2   Move 3

76: Detect the defector

If you solve the nonogram
you find an eye, indicating
the defector is person 2,
as they're wearing an
eye-patch.

77: Rendezvous

As all the postcards feature the Arc Du Triomphe it seems like
that should be the destination, but only one has Meet Here
written on it, and that postcard has one other landmark on it:
The Eiffel Tower.

78: Hidden message

All except four of the books have the title on their spine running
bottom to top. So all you need to do is turn three of the other
books the same way, so that only one book has the title running
top to bottom, and then hide the message in there.

79: Escape the room

The exit doors are monitored by cameras. The chimney has sooty
footprints leaving it so they didn't go out that way. The
placement of the short stepladder indicates they tried to escape
through the skylight but couldn't reach. The screwdriver and
screws on the floor, combined with sooty handprints around the
vent, suggest they left that way, replacing the vent as they went.

80: The barium meal technique

The mole is suspect four. Although it appears canister 3 is missing, you can see that the label for canister 4 is applied slightly lopsided. This is because your fourth suspect removed the label from canister 4 and applied it to canister 3, moving it over to create the deception.

81: Escape the cell

The name you have to strike is Richard. If you extend the lines from the struck out tally marks, it forms a cross, with Richard at the centre.

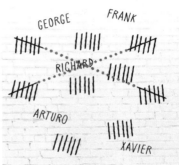

82: Spot the disguise

The man in disguise is in the centre. The other two men's glasses reflect the light, but his don't, indicating that there are no lenses in the frame.

83: Find the safehouse

If you turn your head to the right and look at the shapes, eventually you will be able to discern the number 362.

84: Unlock the box

The paintings give a clue to how to use the number grid. The painting that looks down holds 1 piece of fruit, the one that looks right holds 2, the one looking left holds 3 and the one looking up holds 4.

If you start from the dot and follow the directions when you reach each number, you will draw the following pattern:

This forms the numbers 5.

1	4	2	2	2	2	2	4	4	3
3	1	4	1	3	3	3	3	2	1
4	1	4	2	2	2	2	4	3	4
2	2	4	3	3	3	3	1	1	4
2	4	2	2	2	2	4	1	4	2
1	2	4	3	3	3	3	3	1	1

85: What day?

The agent visited the location at the designated time every day.

86: Choose your poison

You should switch to cocktail B, as counterintuitively you will have a better chance with that one than with cocktail A because the poisoner deliberately revealed one of the poisoned cocktails.

87: Choose your equpment

F: Stocking to disguise face.
L: Tennis ball to distract guard dogs going in.
D: Sling shot to smash spotlights.
C: Spray paint to block out cameras.
B: Hair grip to pick locks.
I: Camera to photo files.
J: Box of matches to destroy files.
G: Beef steak to distract guard dogs going out.

88: Locate the facility

If you plan the routes suggested by drawing lines, then add a cross, as indicated by the icons, you find the real location, Baldwin.

89: Where's Gratzki?

90: Hack the phone

It would be nearly impossible to guess the password, even with the clues you have, but you can see that the phone has FACE-ID active, so you can hold it in front of his face to unlock it.

91: Secret exit

The wall on the left is actually a false wall that conceals a secret exit. The clues to this are the fact that the skirting board does not carry all the way across the left wall and the floorboards seem partially covered by it and the painting on back wall the is not hung in the centre. Since the rest of the room appears so ordered and symmetrical, it doesn't seem likely that the paining would be deliberately hung like that.

92: An enigma
The answer is that unfortunately you should do nothing, as any action will lead to the enemy realizing you have cracked the code.

93: The capsule
The agent should put the poison into the interrogator's water, thereby taking them out of the equation and possibly giving them a chance to escape.

94: Find the phrase
If you use the 10th word from the beginning of the passage and the 4th word before it concludes, you get "red herring", which is incorrect. Instead, you must take the 10th word from the phrase "the start" in the passage, and the 4th word before the phrase "the end", giving you Oxygen White.

95: Exploiting fear
As the enemy is severely arachnophobic, it's not important to select the most frightening-looking or dangerous spider. The priority is which one is you can carry on your person secretly without putting yourself in danger. For this purpose the harvestman is the best spider.

96: Message on a bottle
The third bottle on the second row has the message and a "+" instead of an "&".

97: The mole
Logically, your superior must be the mole. He is the only other person who knew the secret information that ended up in the hands of the enemy.

98: Hornet drone

To crash where it did, the drone must have moved forward, turned right and then moved forward.

That means Forward must be ◉ and Turn Right must be ❖, making ■ represent Turn Left.

Therefore the correct set of instructions to get through the vents is C, which would be F7 TL F2 TL F4 TR F2 TL F3 TR F3.

99: The cipher scenario

The note indicates that you should draw the square shaped C on the note onto the grid, starting from the left-facing arrow and ending at the right facing one. Then, as you follow this path, you decode each of the 26 letters of the message using A or B depending on what is indicated on the grid, e.g. A, A, B, B, A etc. Doing this gives you the message GO TO FIFTEEN RUE DU STAND TWO PM.

100: Orienteering

The map is not indicating a change of location but a change of time. The lines on it represent the hands of a clock, with the shorter line as the hour and the longer the minute. Therefore you should meet your handler at the Guggenheim in Manhattan at 2:25pm.

101: Cryptography

The word key to deciphering the message is THE SPY TEST. Each of the letters in the message has been shifted forward by the number position of each of the letters in the phrase. Here, T is 19th in the alphabet, H is 7th, E is 4th, S is 18th, P is 15th, Y is 24th, E is 4th, S is 18th and T is 19th.

So to decipher you move the first letter back in the alphabet by 19, the second by 7 and so on. When you get to the end you repeat, until the message is revealed:

THIS IS THE END OF THE TEST

Acknowledgements

Alamy Stock Photo: /Universal Images Group North America LLC 23, /CBW 65, /Associated Press 91, /Keystone Press 139 top.

Emma Fraser Reid: 28–29, 44, 54, 70–71, 74, 78–79, 82, 87, 102, 109, 110, 112–113, 115, 125, 129, 133, 136, 150, 148.

iStock / Getty Images Plus: /kprojekt 22, Express / Stringer 121, /pawel-gaul 130 top (t.l., b), Jose Luis Lee 130, borchee 130, Nils Robert 130, /Mark Wilson 139 bottom, / Hulton Deutsch 167 bottom, /John Pierre Rey 167 top.

Shutterstock: 148, /PyTy 27, /Gordon Bell 50–51, / each city 60, /Everett Collection 81, /Christos Georghiou 96–97, / Hein Nouwens 101 top middle, / Morphart Creation 101, / Sina Ettmer Photography 105, /Vasyl Yurlov 124/, /olrat 144–145, /Aleksandr Ozerov 152–153, 156–157.